Almshouses in the
West Riding of Yorkshire
1600–1900

Almshouses in the
West Riding of Yorkshire
1600–1900

Helen Caffrey

Almshouses in the West Riding of Yorkshire: 1600–1900

© Helen Caffrey

ISBN(10) 1-905223-21-8
ISBN(13) 978-1-905223-21-3

Typeset and published 2006 by:

Marketing & Publications Ltd

Hill Farm – Unit F
Castle Acre Road
Great Dunham
King's Lynn
Norfolk, PE32 2LP
Tel: 01760 755645
Fax: 01760 755316
Email: publishing@heritagemp.com
Website: www.heritagemp.com

ACKNOWLEDGEMENTS

Librarians, archivists and curators at the institutions named in the Bibliography have helped in locating documents and illustrations, while trustees, almshouse staff and others have helped with their specific local knowledge. In particular the writer would like to mention:
John Batty (Gawber), Richard Cann (Sedbergh), Peter Cunliffe (Waddington), Ron Firth (Pontefract), Roy Glenn (Wadsley), Angela Hartley (Beamsley), Gaby and Steve Kilburn (Frieston), Charles Kirk (Frieston), Peter Oates (Halifax), Michael Thorley (Hemsworth), Adam White (Aberford) and His Grace the Duke of Norfolk, Arundel Castles, Sussex and the City Librarian, Sheffield (Sheffield).

Shield, crest and niche above the
entrance to the reading room at
Freeman's Hospital. *Photo: author.*

ABBREVIATIONS

BA	Barnsley Archive
BL	Bradford Local Studies Library
CA	Cumbria County Archive
CL	Clitheroe Library
DA	Doncaster Archives
ER	East Riding Archives
HU	Hull University Archive
JG	John Goodchild Collection
LL	Leeds Library and Information Service
NY	North Yorkshire County Record Office
RALS	Rotherham Archive and Local Studies
RL	Ripon Library
SA	Sheffield Archive
TC	Trustee collection
WYAS, B	West Yorkshire Archive Service, Bradford
WYAS, C	West Yorkshire Archive Service, Calderdale
WYAS, K	West Yorkshire Archive Service, Kirklees
WYAS, L	West Yorkshire Archive Service, Leeds
WYAS, W	West Yorkshire Archive Service, Wakefield
WYAS, Y	West Yorkshire Archive Service, Yorkshire Archaeological Society

CONTENTS

LIST OF FIGURES

LIST OF TABLES

PREFACE

One day, exploring an unfamiliar place, I strolled down a ginnel and came upon a small group of houses. They were built in the same local materials as other older buildings in the district, but distinctive in layout and presence. Uniform, behind a flowery border, they were small in scale yet graced with tall chimneys. I took out my notebook to make a sketch.

Some years later, circumstances coalesced to direct me again to such buildings, their inhabitants and purpose. As a group, older people have received little attention from historians, while the poor are more often perceived through legislation. I hope that my work here goes some way to redress the imbalance.

Whilst I have pursued these investigations within one county, I hope that others will extend the study. Poverty in old age may lie ahead for many of us, as it did for past generations. Provision remains as relevant, as do the accompanying social attitudes, values and expectations. Almshouse charities are long-lived: somewhere near you, you may be sure of finding an almshouse.

Helen Caffrey

2006

Chapter 1

Introduction

This investigation into the almshouses of the West Riding arose from two long-term interests: a concern with groups of people under-represented in the historical record, or in the work of other historians, and an application of an archaeological approach to buildings as evidence. This method seeks not only to identify architectural aspects of construction and design but to relate these to function, to look comparatively and quantitatively at a body of material, and to make deductions, however tentatively, about motives and perceptions of builders, occupants and contemporary observers.

The very term 'almshouse' is not always understood, nor indeed was it used consistently in the past. A straightforward definition would be that an almshouse provides charitable accommodation for elderly poor people. By extension, an almshouse charity is, in modern terminology, a residential charity and one that may provide other benefits in addition to a roof overhead. It is also important to realise what an almshouse is not. The problem of the poor and destitute, in particular in response to the dislocation of nineteenth-century industrialisation, attracted attention both then and now so that historians and novelists have contributed to our picture of the poor in the workhouse.

The essential difference is implicit in the words themselves: in a workhouse inmates of whatever age worked for their keep; in an almshouse they received alms, that is charitable support. To go further, the workhouse was the bottom line, the last resort of the destitute; the almshouse residents were selected to benefit from the particular charity, and arguably gained a certain status in so doing. Almshouses were not an official or state response and did not represent any form of governmental attempt to

Fig. 1 Mary Lowther's Hospital. Detail of the central unit with its pediment and foundation plaque. *Photo: author.*

1

cope with social problems. Each almshouse charity was, and indeed is, an individual private charity. In practice this means that while there are essential similarities there are also a good number of differences, sometimes whimsical or even eccentric, between charities.

The other term which may lead to confusion is that of 'hospital'. In the modern sense of course this means a medical institution, while the origins of the word lie alongside those of 'hospitality' and 'hospice'. During the middle ages a hospital's role was to look after those in need of care, whether travellers, the sick, infirm or elderly. What might be seen as isolation hospitals arose, and subsequently declined, to cope with the problem of leprosy. Yet other hospitals were established to cater for the needs of the most vulnerable groups in any society: the poor who were either too young or too old to support themselves financially. Some hospitals were therefore schools (as in the surviving Tudor foundation of Christ's Hospital) while others were dedicated to the elderly. Not a few developed in parallel until changes due to state intervention in the nineteenth century. The next chapter explains these early strands in more detail. Throughout the period the essentially medieval usage of 'hospital' continued as an acceptable alternative to almshouse.

So much for definitions. To look more closely at what almshouses did, their terms of reference, the clientele and their lifestyles, it was found necessary to set certain parameters and to employ a system of classification. These give a framework to study change and continuity over a period notable for changes in the economy, social attitudes and expectations, and in the structure and appearance of buildings. Inevitably there are some grey areas and a few instances which do not fit readily but the categories used have been found adequate for identification of common characteristics and the development of an overall understanding. It is hoped that this will be useful both for social historians and those seeking a context for the specific place or people.

In the first place the Directory given here is for the historic county of the West Riding. It is important to realise that while this provides data on a geographically extensive and populous county, any conclusions drawn may or may not be true for the country as a whole and until such studies are available for far more counties (Lincolnshire and Dorset having received attention so far) and with a similar coverage, general statements should be made with caution. Certainly the West Riding offers a broad canvas in terms of the topographical, economic and social: urban and rural, agriculture, mining, textiles and other industries, varying levels of prosperity, and diversity of religious persuasions which may affect the practical implementation of charity. However, initial investigations (not included here) suggested that expansion to, say, Hull and the coast, and to the city of York, would introduce other factors and responses within Yorkshire, just as in the national scene almshouses provided by trade associations and London livery companies affect the charitable landscape of the Home Counties.

It has been an especial concern here to establish a factual basis secured to the data and to consider interpretation only in the light of evidence. This is essential where conclusions arising from this study do not coincide with popular or general knowledge of the subject, or those brief passing comments, handed on from one historian to the next.

For the most part, the material here covers the period from after the Reformation until the run-up to the Welfare State, in round terms three centuries from 1600 to 1900. The almshouses extant during this period include some earlier foundations and a few re-foundations. They also include cases where the accommodation was rebuilt, not necessarily on the same site, and other changes took place in the way in which the charity was implemented. Some of these could certainly be understood as 'modernisation' and accordingly seen in a more or less favourable light alongside the 'traditional'. Such changes place a charity within the wider historical scene and give a genuine taste of attitudes and expectations. A final reminder should be given of the distinction between almshouse building and almshouse charity. In the present century many historic charities continue to function but because of changes both demographic and legislative these may no longer be residential or may be relocated in buildings similar to those of other providers of housing appropriate to the requirements of older people.

The interface between state provision and the variously labelled forms of provision of the private or voluntary sector is addressed very briefly in Chapter Two, but merits further attention to identify particular groups targeted and choices made; also to acknowledge a debt. Earlier charitable foundations offered models for 'new' state provision, while the continued existence of the former might equally continue to offer lessons to the latter.

The following Chapters Three and Four explain how the buildings have been classified and why, who lived there and how they were chosen, and how the charities were funded and regulated. The discussion offers both background and foreground to almshouse life within the longer historical context, before and after 1600–1900, set out in Chapter Two. The Directory is given alphabetically by town or village; the numbers which appear in square brackets in these chapters refer to those entries in the Directory. All almshouse charities in existence or known to have existed previously at the time of the Charity Commissioners' survey in the 1890s are listed, with particular attention given to extant almshouse buildings.

More is said later about the Charity Commissioners (predecessors of the present Charity Commission). Their reports were invaluable in compiling the Directory, but the issues which concerned them most – accountability, financial rectitude and clarity; good practice and a measure of standardisation – are not the focus of this investigation. The five substantial volumes occupied by the assorted endowed charities of the West Riding cover a fascinating range of charitable endeavour. They also indicate the parochial and customary nature of many small charities and the difficulties of tracking down written confirmation. Only in a few cases – often arising from the public enquiries held by the visiting inspectors – do any intimate details emerge of almshouse life and living standards, and the opinions of officials and interested locals.

This writer also experienced problems in tracing written sources, not on account of any overall shortage of material on the subject but because of its uneven and haphazard coverage. Some charities maintained impeccable records, notably minute books kept by the trustees' clerk, subsequently deposited in their local archive or still in the care of the trustees. Other documents have made their way individually into the fourteen record offices and are so disparate as to offer only a tantalising vignette of a particular incident or point in time. Not surprisingly, the exceptional, whether a rebuilding

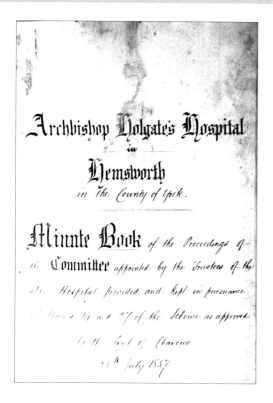

Fig. 2 Archbishop Holgate's Hospital. The minute book of the Buildings Committee, set up in 1857 to oversee the rebuilding project, records supplementary advice to tendering architects based on residents' relative status and the funds allocated. *WYAS, W, C345/1/6.*

project or accusations of embezzlement, are accorded the most detailed reporting. The almspeople themselves leave only a slight written trace. This is partly a reflection of literacy levels, partly a feature of that 'historical invisibility' which prompted this work. However, though few numerically, from the mid-nineteenth century and increasingly into the early twentieth individual letters, forms or note of personal circumstances survive from those applying to the charity.

Some of these make harrowing reading, although they have to be read in the light of their times. They give, if not a face, at least a name, age and sometimes occupation to the individual. It is this material, in conjunction with the trustees' decisions (although not, alas, the reasons for most of those decisions) that gives substance to the social group from which almshouse residents were generally selected, and which might be more narrowly defined than the original specifications of the founder. From this emerges an image of what was intended and to some extent what was done (discussed in Chapter Four).

The buildings also reflect the people concerned, and in a complementary dimension. They demonstrate the provision considered appropriate to the way of life and status of almspeople, and contemporary understanding of the needs of the elderly. They may display a dichotomy between space and facilities experienced inside and the public face of an architectural façade. The whole has to be set within the local community and within the scope of the housing available to their peers; the munificence of the founder is symbiotic with the importance of philanthropy and the status of the elderly residents who have achieved this accolade. Approached in this way, the buildings are

Fig. 3 Residents at Beamsley Hospital, undated photograph. *Craven Herald and Pioneer.*

5

far more than a pretty face or quaint feature. The viewer may come to achieve some realisation of a specific genre of architecture which is not only readily recognisable but physically embodies particular values and messages. Contemporary viewers may have 'read' these as they were intended, subtexts and all. It is harder to do so with certainty from a different perspective on the hierarchical society, measures for social control and the deserving and undeserving poor.

It is hoped that this Directory may appeal to those who have an enquiring mind and concern for the human condition as well as a compulsion to see 'the real thing' and test out ideas for themselves. While the Directory may give a new dimension to places seen about the West Riding, that essential element of the almshouse charity remains vital: the dignity of the residents. The writer encountered many friendly people, delighted to talk about their homes, and so, if visiting, please remember that almshouses are just that.

Chapter 2

Context

While it is never possible to 'start at the beginning' and 'stop at the end' in any organic historical investigation the curious reader may wish to know a little more about medieval origins and twentieth-century developments before approaching the buildings themselves. It will be seen that previous research has emphasised the medieval and architectural. Sources for further reading are listed in the Bibliography.

After Rotha Mary Clay's seminal work in 1909, medieval almshouses (1070–1570) have been studied by Nicholas Orme and Margaret Webster with a particular interest in Devon and Cornwall; by Patricia Cullum whose thesis concentrates on Yorkshire; and E.C. Prescott covering the extended period of 1200–1640. Almshouse architecture (as distinct from 'buildings') terminating in the eighteenth century was the focus of W. Godfrey's work in 1955, followed by Brian Howson in 1993 with some useful material on later almshouses. W.K. Jordan's great work on charity during the period 1480–1660 includes a regional case study for Yorkshire containing a section on almshouses. Two other theses focus on the seventeenth century: S. Lambert in Berkshire challenging Jordan's model of rise and decline, and P. Hunnyball considering charitable buildings in Hertfordshire as an expression of social status. The West Riding is still dependent on the 1913 edition for the Victoria County History, which gives some coverage for early foundations, while the most recent county study is Linda Crust's survey for Lincolnshire.

A few almshouses have generated individual histories, and certainly there is material for plenty more. Work by Richard Cann at Sedbergh and J. Roach in Sheffield is relevant here, and in York, Georgian almshouses have attracted the attention of Elizabeth Brunskill while Cullum has investigated the medieval St. Leonard's Hospital. Within the West Riding almshouses have featured in some town and village studies, again with the emphasis on the architecturally distinguished. T.D. Whitaker's notable work on Craven included some personal observations on Fountain's Hospital, while Mary Bridge's local history of Waddington treats its almshouse in depth. Wakefield and its environs were closely observed by W. S. Banks in 1871 and a century later by Kate Taylor for European Architectural Heritage Year, 1976. Finally, there have always been commentators concerned with the performance of charities: accountability, transparency and adherence to the foundation's aims. Doncaster's charities were thoroughly investigated by C. Jackson in 1881, while in the East Riding Thomas White carried out an enquiry into the almshouses in Hull in 1833, based on personal experience as an overseer of the poor. Such investigations demonstrate changes that have occurred since foundation as well as contemporary perceptions of the almshouse role.

Early foundations

So what can be said of the origins of the almshouse in England? It would seem that medieval hospitals (as they should be called) were essentially controlled and run by clerics, either as part of a monastic complex or standing alone. These establishments might well be supported financially by sufficiently prosperous and caring members of the aristocracy who were concerned with their salvation, and who thereby had a say in the functions of the hospital. This might include some provision for the household's retainers in their old age while guilds may have taken on similar responsibility for their members. As early as 680, Bede saw the infirm and those close to death receiving care in the monastery at Whitby and a sprinkling of tenth and eleventh century references indicate Athelstan, Eadred and Lanfranc making provision for the care of the elderly and infirm, beyond any purely personal arrangements (Orme and Webster, 1995).

No clear distinction appears in early hospitals between religious and medical care and the benefit of a roof over one's head: the consolations were complementary. The group who were treated (or at least accommodated) separately, on grounds of the risk of infection, were lepers. Of the 68 hospitals known for England between the mid-eleventh and the mid-twelfth centuries, Orme and Webster found half to be leper houses. The disease mercifully waned until redundant houses found new uses; in 1342 St. Mary Magdalene in Ripon [82] was a home for blind priests. While the client group for hospitals continued to be the poor, sick and disabled, without age specified, travellers and pilgrims, among the original clientele, declined in numbers, perhaps suggesting a distinction between temporary and long-term needs. The hospital of St. John the Baptist in Ripon [81] may have been a resting place for pilgrims but now supported four or five poor clerics who kept school in Ripon, while food was distributed there to paupers requesting alms (Cullum, 1989). A diminished population and economic dislocation following the Black Death of 1348–49 may account for some hospital closures in the later fourteenth century, possibly twenty percent of houses (Orme and Webster, 1995).

But fluctuation was not new and records are sparse. Cullum has identified a category of Yorkshire foundations, more often called maisondewes (a variant of maisonsdieu) that proliferated during the fourteenth to fifteenth century. These were characteristically small, urban and often unendowed. Rather than being dismissed as inadequate these charities might be understood as a short-term form of provision, and one where beneficiaries were also more likely to move on. The fortunate resident of this rent-free accommodation could support him or herself by begging – seen as socially acceptable in these circumstances – or might be the recipient of some small charitable bequest such as a gown (Cullum, 1989).

Two strands in the later history of almshouses appear during the fourteenth century: a concern for the proper governance of 'xenodochia, leprosarie, eleemosynarie and hospitalia' (as expressed by Pope Clement V: 'guest houses, lazar houses, almshouses and hospices') and for fuller provision for the needs of the poor. The Lollards' manifesto of 1395, certainly a political document, went beyond attacking clerical abuse to make recommendations: the current one hundred almshouses were insufficient, and a further hundred plus fifteen universities could be established through the redirection of funding from religious institutions. In 1414 the Commons petitioned for an enquiry. Dissatisfaction over improper use of resources intended for the poor continued to be an issue until overtaken (temporarily) by the dissolution of religious houses.

Most medieval hospitals, like their successors, were small foundations, providing between four and thirteen beds. These were typically arranged in cubicles down both sides of a long ward, possibly with a chapel in view at one end, although later these were usually detached. Some trends observed in Chapter Three for the sixteenth to seventeenth century had their roots in changes of the fourteenth to fifteenth century as there was 'a rising emphasis on individual privacy in dwellings' and 'communal life was increasingly restricted to the chapel and sometimes a dining hall and kitchen; separate rooms replaced the dormitories of the past' (Orme and Webster, 1995). Alongside this went a preference for cash allowances over communal meals. But while new foundations were more likely to embrace new approaches, not all were ready to move away from the religious environment where almspeople and nurses/servants were accompanied by clerical beneficiaries, corrodians (privileged retainers) enjoying free accommodation and, as in the chantries, those funded to say prayers in perpetuity for the souls of founders and donors. Such a separation of functions and ideas may have been far less clearcut at the time.

Nevertheless another trend that may have been in place before the Reformation was the increasing secularisation of hospitals. A clue may lie in the names, as founders were favoured in place of saints (although the Directory shows a number of seventeenth-century examples where these happily coincide). Meanwhile by the early sixteenth century urban foundations were likely to be run by municipal corporations or guilds. If the religious: secular balance remains uncertain, what could be claimed is a greater institutional diversity alongside more specialisation of function. The identification of the elderly as appropriate recipients of charity appeared in Robert Copland's poem *The Highway to the Spitalhouse* written about 1530. These are the people who 'for their living can do no labour / And have them friends to do them succour / As old people sick and

Fig. 4 Ruins of the fourteenth century hospital chapel of St. Anne's, Ripon. A hall, with wards for men and women, and two small rooms for the resident priest (recorded by Rev. Lukis in 1879) occupied the present garden. The current almshouse, built 1869, occupies the former hospital garden to the right of the photo. *Photo: author.*

impotent' (Judges, 1936). Copland also discussed the problem of distinguishing the deserving from the undeserving poor, by no means a new concept, but here applied to the almshouse.

Henry VIII's legislation during the 1530s and 1540s reduced the number of functioning hospitals, however anomalous and inconsistent its application. The *Valor Ecclesiasticus* sought to distinguish between hospitals run by the clergy and those whose aim was the distribution of alms in accordance with the wishes of the founder. Targets for closure moved from small, arguably unviable, institutions, to chantries, then some larger hospitals and collegiate churches. Plans to use the funds released in the provision of new free grammar schools and increased support for the poor and elderly were dissipated by the rapid changes of government following Henry's death, as were the funds themselves.

Reinvention and new patrons

But not all pre-Reformation almshouses were shut down or went into voluntary liquidation. The Knolles Hospital at Pontefract [73] is a case in point, as its collegiate status made it vulnerable. Founded in 1385 by Robert and Constance Knolles, this was a lay foundation, but traditional in form. The establishment consisted of a master, six chaplains, two clerks and thirteen 'feeble poor who had been brought to destitution by misfortune' and two servants to care for them. Constance may have been the originator of the project, a native of Pontefract but not resident since her marriage to Robert. The couple were probably childless as the bulk of their estate went to make up the endowment. The substantial annual sum of £102. 10s. 7d. covered the payments of 20 marks to the master, 10 to each chaplain, 5 to each clerk, 2 to each of the servants, with the balance feeding and clothing the 'feeble poor' plus treats on feast days (Cullum, 1989, 355).

The Knolles Hospital (ironically later known as Trinities from its proximity to that church) survived the Dissolution, as did other local establishments, taken into the care of the corporation. Its medieval layout lasted until the mid-nineteenth century, as Fox described the common room, church and 'many mansions for the poor' set in a 'square entered through a wooden gatehouse' (Fox, 1827). More surprisingly, the Ripon almshouses [80–82] continued, St. Anne's subsequently refounded by the corporation, but St. John's and St. Mary Magdalene, undeniably ecclesiastical, continued as almshouses to be later amalgamated and remain a rare example today of church control, under the jurisdiction of the bishop of Ripon (Y/362 900; Pearson, 1972). One can only assume there were friends in high places and that effective networking took place. A few other survivals may be found in the Directory, perhaps escaping due to insignificance. Little is known of the process of refoundation and whether more than a memory remained by the following century. Ironically, three new foundations – at Hemsworth, Kirkthorpe and possibly Darfield [41, 49, 20] – were funded from wealth privately acquired as a result of the Dissolution.

During her relatively brief reign Mary Tudor encouraged the refoundation of some high-profile hospitals, then Elizabeth's Church Settlement of 1559 established the principle of tax exemption for charity to the poor, policed by visitations. The subsequent growth of almshouse charities among others was recognised in 1598 by

Fig. 5 Arksey. The almshouses provided by local benefactor Bryan Cooke in 1660. *Photo: author.*

legislation permitting incorporation with a common seal and endowments of up to £200 per annum. Further legislation facilitated foundation without parliamentary consent as previously required. It should be remembered that Elizabeth's government did make serious attempts to tackle the problems of poverty and recognition of the scale of the problem made charitable endeavour even more valuable. By this time almshouse charities were constitutionally set on the lines they follow in the succeeding centuries.

Jordan (1961) has described the earlier seventeenth century as a 'period of amazing generosity and social sensitivity'. Outstanding among examples of generosity in Yorkshire was Nathaniel Waterhouse [39] a Halifax salter who gave a total of £3,304. 9s. to a number of social, educational and religious charities including the well-endowed almshouses (now in modern premises as the Waterhouse Homes). The even greater sum of £3,820 was bequeathed by Bryan Cooke of Arksey [5] a barrister and country gentleman who died unmarried, aged only 41. But to the elderly poor man or woman it was local availability that mattered. It has been estimated that by 1660 there were 83 enduring almshouses and 29 short-term or unendowed foundations functioning across Yorkshire (Jordan, 1961). As evidence of generosity this is truly admirable, but as a solution to need, to population distribution, and to an expanding population, it was quite inadequate. Chance – in living within an almshouse catchment area – was a factor in eligibility. But where there was a presence, this visible and permanent form of provision also served to keep the needs of the elderly poor within public consciousness.

No major cataclysms affected almshouses within the period 1600–1900, although external trends undoubtedly influenced maintenance and development and within this some foundations were more vulnerable than others. The state of uncertainty arising from the civil wars of the mid-seventeenth century and a post-war economy struggling with reconstruction had an adverse effect on charities whose endowments depended on rent charges on land or residential property. However no examples have been found of serious decline or closure directly attributable to this or to later agricultural depressions. Nor did the state of the economy have any obvious impact on the rate of foundation; individual bequests were discrete instances of philanthropy, based upon an accumulation of prosperity. Table 1 shows the rate of foundation persisting through the seventeenth and eighteenth centuries. The latter saw some change of direction for the charitable impulse as new challenges were tackled and more effort was collective in the

11

form of associations (Checkland, 1980). For almshouses this phase could be seen as one of continuity and consolidation.

Table 1 Date of foundation, by century for all almshouses in the Directory

Pre-1600	1601–1700	1701–1800	1801–1901	Uncertain
14	26	28	38	9

Philanthropists and bureaucracy

During the nineteenth century almshouse charity gathered momentum both in terms of new foundations and improvement, expansion and rebuilding amongst those already established. As always, individual motivation was both personal and complex but now expressed within a context of attempts to combat or contain poverty through the New Poor Law of 1834, a government-imposed application of local bureaucracy based upon the principle of less eligibility. As classification of the deserving and undeserving poor hardened, and workhouses were welcomed (by those outside) as a final solution, the distinctive role of almshouses appealed to philanthropic Victorians. Rather than being perceived as outdated or irrelevant, their personal form of charity on a human scale attracted supplementary bequests and some new and ambitious projects, indicated in the following two chapters. Claims for the supremacy of the medieval or Tudor-Stuart almshouse may be eclipsed by those of the nineteenth century as private charity thrived alongside official intervention.

Two new factors were at work, stimulating and influencing the nature of provision. The first was location as demographic changes arising from the industrial revolution left an enlarged poverty-stricken population in the cities, after their useful working life had ended. The erratic distribution of almshouses had never reflected population, Bradford, for example, having no almshouses before 1845, but four [11–14] being built in the following thirty years. Sheffield and Leeds, each with at least one substantial earlier charity, increased their provision through a number of new foundations. Halifax, already a successful textile town with relatively generous facilities for the poor, now constructed new almshouses as part of its outpouring of affluence in both public and domestic building.

The second change was in the knowledge base. Previously charitable endeavour might be based on personal observation and, sometimes, familiarity with the local community and its circumstances. Now the enthusiasm for classification and statistics provided not only evidence for poverty and deprivation but a clearer understanding of its place in the life cycle and relationship with health and other social issues. The work of Booth (quoted in Chapter Four), other dedicated individuals and government commissions supplied a backbone to legislation on public health, housing, education and working conditions. The very extent of the problem revealed fuelled the distinction between the deserving and undeserving poor as a guide to the allocation of resources. Moral and religious enthusiasm (as evinced, for example, by the Salvation Army) reached out towards those who, if not manifestly deserving, might become so.

These attitudes were social rather than sectarian. The wealthy and successful, with the means to be charitable, now included an increasing number of business people who

Fig. 6 Joseph Crossley's Almshouses in Halifax, completed by his son Edward in 1870. *Photo: author.*

were non-conformists, frequently Methodists. Their contribution to the West Riding, especially its industrial towns and cities, was both economic and philanthropic. The Crossley family [36, 37] in Halifax reinvested the profits of their carpet manufacture so as to benefit business, themselves and their employees. The town centre received a rational street layout, a public park was created, the chapel beautified, orphanage (later school) established, improved housing built for the workforce and mansions for the Crossleys, and two sets of almshouses established for a total of seventy retired workers or other needy elderly people (Bretton, 1950–54). The range of amenities demonstrates not only wealth but a holistic approach, in tune with the contemporary interest in model settlements and communities. Titus Salt's magnificent creation of Saltaire also included almshouses [84] and a cottage hospital, the particular interest of his wife Caroline. It is no coincidence that the two families were linked by marriage.

Another peripheral development that impinged upon some almshouses was the state's responsibility for education. After the 1870 Education Act pupil movements led to a gradual decline in most of the small schools within the combined charities. In practical terms this meant that the school building became solely a home for the schoolmaster or mistress, or was used as a community room or Sunday school, later being converted to additional almshouse places. Where the school became large and successful, the older buildings were outgrown, a new site found and the almshouse left behind. The main effect on the almshouses – apart from peace and quiet for the residents – lay in the reapportionment of the charity's resources between the two functions.

While the rebuilding and expansion of almshouses incorporated elements of modernity and historicism, as discussed in Chapter Three, refoundation also had some curious features. Does the renamed St. Leonard's Hospital at Horbury [44] indicate the state of decay of the original charity, a religious consciousness (appropriate to the home of *Onward Christian Soldiers*) or an invocation of a non-existent medieval religious ancestry? The Victorian appreciation of the past might be employed to lay claim to an enduring future. Horbury is interesting too in its inclusion of another modern feature: an attached cottage, symbolically set back at right-angles to the row of four, for the district nurse. The community roles of official and private welfare provision had become inter-linked.

The trends and changes of these three centuries have been observed through the buildings and documents of the almshouse charities. Not surprisingly, more has survived from the nineteenth century relating to both new and earlier foundations. As secondary sources were discussed at the beginning of this chapter it is now time to assess the resources underpinning Chapters Three and Four. The Introduction indicated some of the problems encountered in tracking down material (not least that in locating sites from directions given a century ago)! Especially useful among the documents are the trustees' minute books, accounts and registers. Wills should be mentioned where these constituted foundation documents, and a good number of these have survived from the seventeenth century, the Beaumont material having been preserved in both final and draft form (DDCA (2) 11; DDCA 4). A rare chronicle, unfortunately unfinished, for the Archbishop Holgate Hospital was undertaken by its master, Mr. Armstrong (C 345/1/26), while official records include the Gilbert returns of 1786 identifying current charities and the much more extensive records of the Charity Commissioners, embodying two sets of published volumes (1837 and 1897–99) with individual reports and a rehearsal of earlier evidence, no longer all available. Cross-referencing sometimes allows changes to be pinpointed, as at the Earl of Shrewsbury's Hospital where the original form of governance was arbitrarily altered by Lady Mary Howard during her son's minority, replacing a senior brother with a clerical manager. Occasionally the abandonment of earlier customs, such as provision of clothing, may be deduced, at least by their absence. Into the twentieth century, an increasing number of official bodies has become involved, giving rise to further reports on selected aspects of the charities' workings. Amongst all this the buildings present an unequivocal statement of intentions, with regulations and admission criteria to aid our interpretation. Present day residents and trustees are a valuable source not only for the present but with long memories of things seen and said by their predecessors.

Contemporary perceptions

Some of that may be hearsay, which in itself has the merit of reflecting popular perceptions. It might be hoped that these would appear in the literary and artistic record, but this is disappointing: slight overall and non-existent for the West Riding. Nevertheless three novelists of national standing did feature almshouses in their books: Thomas Peacock (1785–1866), Charles Dickens (1812–70) and Anthony Trollope (1815–82). Peacock satirised bureaucracy, ever a satisfying target and a sector in which he himself worked. *Crotchet Castle* written in 1831 gave a humorous account of an inspector's enquiries into an apparently defunct charity. Responsible people and ancient inhabitants were questioned as the receipt of the annual sum due to the charity, one penny, was taken seriously. This had more to say about attitudes to officialdom than to almshouses, but showed the Charity Commissioners' processes prior to their first reports.

Dickens and Trollope shared a concern over abuses that must be brought to public attention and, as novelists, with human nature and the development of their characters. Trollope's novel *The Warden*, (See Chapter Four), was influential but did not reflect the almshouse norm so much as an establishment response to corruption, scapegoats and whistle-blowing. Dickens did not set any of his novels within an almshouse (an environment surely begging his attention) but described a couple of visits in *Household Words* (1850–59) and the *Uncommercial Traveller* (first published with the former and later reissued by popular demand). The investigative journalist took his reader to places of interest to witness quaint customs and contemporary institutions. Both establishments, one rural, the other, 'Titbull's', based on many in London, passed muster. Considering his outspoken treatment of schools, what is significant is that no malpractice appeared here.

Historical and topographical writers (notably Whitaker and Banks) illustrated the occasional almshouse building, but not their interiors or activities demonstrating their function. Surely the physiognomy of life experience would appeal to portrait painters? But who would commission or purchase such works? Frans Hals painted the *Regents and Regentesses of the Almshouses* at Haarlem (Frans Hals Museum, Haarlem) in 1664–65, when he was himself in his eighties and living in poverty, as two corporate group portraits; but these were the boards of trustees, not the residents. The Regentesses were serious elderly women, their portraits conveying both conscientious endeavour and a sense of humanity despite severity of dress. In 1872 Frederick Walker (1830–75) painted the garden of the historic Jesus Hospital at Bray, Berkshire, as *The Harbour of Refuge* (Tate Gallery, London). Compositionally unbalanced it did show the residents' use of the garden, although dominated by a youthful carer and gardener symbolic of the grim reaper. Walker favoured set-piece character studies and achieved fame for his theatre posters.

Very different was Hubert von Herkomer (1849–1914) a painter of powerful scenes of working people's lives. He is mentioned here, not as a painter of an almshouse, but for his depiction of elderly women in a workhouse – probably St. James's, Westminster – in *Eventide* (Walker Art Gallery, Liverpool) in 1876. The scene is not unduly grim nor the institution demonised or sentimentalised, but despite the homely drinking of tea women are struggling to sew or sit vacantly, all together in one large room. The artist himself commented on their 'often childish work' and that 'the agony of threading their needles was affecting indeed' (Morris, 1996). This was the alternative happily avoided by almswomen.

After 1900

The final part of this chapter continues the historical context for almshouses after the period of this study, through the twentieth century, as more charities were founded and others continued and developed. This brief overview does not imply any less significance; the topic awaits further study.

In 1908 Lloyd George, then Chancellor in Asquith's government, brought in the non-contributory old age pension of 5s. per week at age 70. This was collected at the pensioner's local post office and entirely distinct from poor relief and the stigma of the Poor Law. The extent of uptake surprised the government; as Lloyd George said it revealed 'a mass of poverty and destitution which is too proud to wear the badge of pauperism' (Fraser, 2003). Restrictions, carrying lingering echoes of the deserving versus undeserving poor, were removed and eligibility extended. The impact on pensioners' lives was recorded by Flora Thompson in *Lark Rise to Candleford* as she herself had seen it from behind the post office counter: 'life was transformed for such aged cottagers. They were relieved of anxiety. They were suddenly rich. Independent for life! They would say as they picked up their money, 'God bless that Lord George – and God bless you, miss"(Thompson, 1939, 97).

While pensions reduced the threat of poverty in old age, the Housing and Town Planning Act enabled local authorities to obtain government subsidies towards the building of council houses for the respectable working classes. Initially intended for the employed and their families, council housing proliferated following the slum clearances of the 1930s and 1950s. As well as family houses and flats, small clusters of bungalows were built for elderly people, often grouped about a small green. Rents had to be paid but assistance in the form of reduced rates and later Housing Benefit placed them within the reach of far more pensioners. Life expectancy increased post-War, supported by health care and prescriptions funded by the National Health Service with a rise in living standards for many.

Almshouses meanwhile continued and new ones were founded. Occasionally the discerning 'customer' might be in a position to choose whether to apply to a charity or the local authority (pers. com.) but the ratio of demand to availability maintained waiting lists. The rosy picture was offset by other factors, especially since the 1980 'right to buy' Housing Act reduced the stock of council housing, although excluding any accommodation specifically for the infirm or disabled. Housing Associations became major providers of social housing, some focusing on older people's needs by providing improvement grants to prolong independence. A halfway house between the family home and institutional care was promoted as sheltered housing, a concept already familiar to almshouse charities.

Political and economic circumstances in the later twentieth century produced another government initiative, Care in the Community, whereby undesirable institutionalisation and occupation of hospital beds were to be avoided through voluntary support by friends, neighbours and relatives for those who could no longer manage entirely on their own. Carers have always been with us, but at last became a recognised body, although the extent of caring identified by the 2001 census came as a shock. The traditional almshouse requirement that an applicant should be one with no alternative support system comes to mind as does the family struggle and sacrifice where no such charity was present. Meanwhile care homes, old people's homes and nursing homes offering institutional provision continued to reflect the vagaries and fashions of the century. An increasing elderly population and financial incentives offered a business opportunity to their directors, until further regulation and economic factors reversed the trend. The communal approach (popularly understood as everyone sitting blankly about a loud TV) has lost favour to a larger element of privacy and a range of activities.

Alongside local authority, RSLs (that is, other social landlords) and private provision, almshouse charities have maintained their distinctive contribution. Some common factors have impacted upon all providers, notably longevity and the ageing population. This may have a particular effect on charities whose founders specified age requirements: not only has our definition of old age shifted, but some almshouse charities actually need a lower minimum age to suit younger people whose special needs are considered to bring them within their remit (pers. com.). There are still more women residents than men, but strict criteria based on local boundaries and church attendance may no longer be realistic or seem a true reflection of the founder's generous intentions. Perhaps 'of good conversation' (see Chapter Four) is still relevant, if hard to translate.

Constraints may also affect those eligible to be trustees, even though individuals prepared to give their time and expertise voluntarily remain at a premium. Pace and complexity of legislation have also increased as building regulations, health and safety measures, disability entitlements and historic building controls present new and sometimes conflicting challenges. The installation of central heating, double glazing or hand rails to front doors may be difficult issues (pers. com.). Where problems seem intractable the options are sale and rebuild or internal conversion. Financial pressures led a significant number of almshouse charities to utilise the 1974 Housing Act to change their status to that of housing association, enabling them to charge a modest rent to recoup expenses and keep up maintenance. Figures from the late 1990s show this solution declining in popularity for smaller almshouses (Pannell and Thomas, 1999).

It may be that present (2005) society recognises the perceived needs and contribution of older people through the provision of bus passes and free TV licences; a pension system is still in place. Yet state support has been paralleled by an increase in services offered by specialist charities, both national and local. Predictions do not suit the historian, but at the very least an ageing population and eroding pensions indicate the continuing relevance of almshouse charities.

Three examples are now considered briefly as indications of the scope and instances of continuity and change within almshouses in the West Riding in the twentieth century. The Cottage Homes at Netherton near Huddersfield opened in 1910, five years before the demise of their founder, millowner Alfred Sykes. When the first minuted meeting was held plans were already well advanced and trustees only needed to choose between red tiles or grey slate for the roof, to accept the draft trust deed and rules and agree on a date to lay the foundation stone. Five was not perhaps the most 'traditional' number of units, as shown in Chapter Three, but with two residents in each, ten may have seemed orderly. Three of the original almspeople were accompanied by a daughter, one by his wife, and the other by another almsman who was paid 5s. for caretaking duties. Coal was supplied (until conversion to gas) and food and medical charges for sick residents were paid by the charity. In 1918 a seriously ill resident received 15s. a week as her daughter gave up work to care for her, but when the carer died the survivor had to leave as 'no other relations would undertake to look after her' (KC 992/2). The local appointment of a district nurse in 1920 suggested a good use for a vacant almshouse but in practice the overlap of two administrative systems made this less satisfactory.

What has changed with the century? Plaques and inscriptions, discussed further in the next chapter, may be significant. Here the term 'cottage homes' has replaced that of almshouse, but if that was to avoid any negative connotations of charity the familiar appearance of the single-storey stone row reaffirmed its status. The two plaques stressed the importance of family and continuity whilst modestly omitting the founder's name: 'Honour thy father and thy mother. These cottage-homes were built in memory of his parents by a son. They were opened by a grandson; the cornerstone was laid by a great-grandson'. The charity has continued to attract grants for improvements whilst expressing ambivalence over the payment of rent by the residents (pers. com.).

Other twentieth-century almshouses may be found across the county, but what has become of some older foundations? Pontefract was aware of its ancient responsibilities in 1854, referring to the 'imperative duty of the corporate body' towards these 'monuments of our pious ancestors' (Jefferson, 1854) and thirty years later became an early example of an amalgamated charity – an approach which became the flavour of the month in the 1950s. But Pontefract did not stand still and in 1913 a maltster, WJ Robson, built four more almshouses below the castle in a traditional row plus pediment but with detailing reminiscent of library architecture of the period, while further benefactions led to the building of eight (now eleven) units on Ryder Close, near to the rebuilt Thwaite's and Ward's Hospitals [76, 77]. Old buildings have been replaced, sometimes as groupings on new sites funded by property rents from the old ones: a very traditional approach to almshouse endowment. The charity now administers 26 units, accommodating up to 35 residents; criteria are prior local residence and the payment of a small contribution that does not change their status as almspeople (pers. com.). Continuity was recently demonstrated by the receipt of a legacy due to compulsory purchase of some London property: it transpired that this originated in a will made in 1574, as beneficial now as then.

The final example comes from Bradford, mentioned previously as a latecomer to almshouse foundation. It may be said to have caught up in the twentieth century through the foundation of the Flower Fund Homes. Innovation here lay in funding rather than in provision. In 1957 Ernest Marrlott, Bradford businessman, proposed the introduction of a Swedish idea whereby floral offerings at funerals would be replaced by charitable donations in cash – later common practice – towards a specific fund to establish homes for the elderly 'of slender means'. By the mid-1970s there were five Homes, small communities each of about twenty people, from Flower Bank costing £26,000 to Flower Hill, and more in the 1990s. A familiar pattern of groups of bungalows about a maintained garden (or three single-storey ranges in a courtyard layout) provided a way of 'housing elderly people sensibly so that they can enjoy a simple life in a small compact home with all the modern conveniences and look after themselves as long as they are well enough to do so' (Bradford Telegraph and Argus, 1971).

In technical terms the Homes are both a registered charity and a housing association but conceptually they lie within the almshouse tradition, supported by elements of public subscription, grants and local authority support. Plans for Flower Bank, 1960, show pairs of units each comprising a 12 x 12 ft (360 x 360 cm) living room beside a 10 x 12 ft (300 x 360 cm) bedroom with inset cupboards, porch and fireplace; kitchen, bathroom and fuel store adjoin the rear. The selection of quiet and spacious sites, yet close to the amenities, reflects a pattern shown in Chapter Three. Even the origins of the Flower Fund echo those of many almshouses as commemorative, arising from a bereavement in the founder's family extended by many small donors contributing 'a rose for the living' as the Fund's motto proclaims.

It is hard to ascertain the extent of almshouse provision at the beginning of the twenty first century. The Almshouse Association (2003) recorded a national membership of 1771 charities housing 35,483 residents, and lists 99 member charities within West Riding (2005). As this is not a comprehensive list, any more than that of the Charity

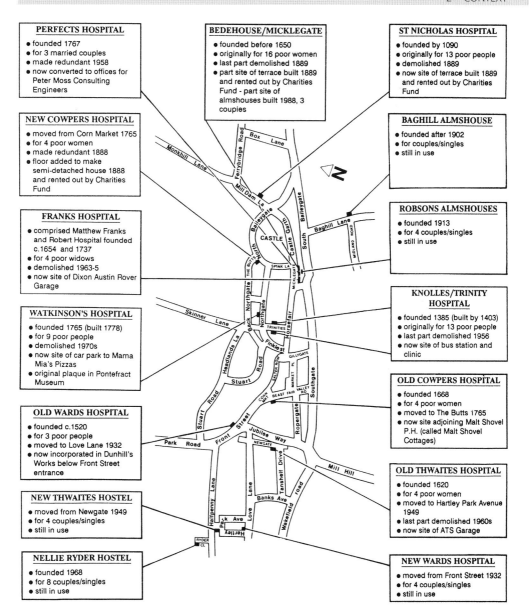

PERFECTS HOSPITAL
- founded 1767
- for 3 married couples
- made redundant 1958
- now converted to offices for Peter Moss Consulting Engineers

NEW COWPERS HOSPITAL
- moved from Corn Market 1765
- for 4 poor women
- made redundant 1888
- floor added to make semi-detached house 1888 and rented out by Charities Fund

FRANKS HOSPITAL
- comprised Matthew Franks and Robert Hospital founded c.1654 and 1737
- for 4 poor widows
- demolished 1963-5
- now site of Dixon Austin Rover Garage

WATKINSON'S HOSPITAL
- founded 1765 (built 1778)
- for 9 poor people
- demolished 1970s
- now site of car park to Mama Mia's Pizzas
- original plaque in Pontefract Museum

OLD WARDS HOSPITAL
- founded c.1520
- for 3 poor people
- moved to Love Lane 1932
- now incorporated in Dunhill's Works below Front Street entrance

NEW THWAITES HOSTEL
- moved from Newgate 1949
- for 4 couples/singles
- still in use

NELLIE RYDER HOSTEL
- founded 1968
- for 8 couples/singles
- still in use

BEDEHOUSE/MICKLEGATE
- founded before 1650
- originally for 16 poor women
- last part demolished 1889
- part site of terrace built 1889 and rented out by Charities Fund - part site of almshouses built 1988, 3 couples

ST NICHOLAS HOSPITAL
- founded by 1090
- originally for 13 poor people
- demolished 1889
- now site of terrace built 1889 and rented out by Charities Fund

BAGHILL ALMSHOUSE
- founded after 1902
- for couples/singles
- still in use

ROBSONS ALMSHOUSES
- founded 1913
- for 4 couples/singles
- still in use

KNOLLES/TRINITY HOSPITAL
- founded 1385 (built by 1403)
- originally for 13 poor people
- last part demolished 1956
- now site of bus station and clinic

OLD COWPERS HOSPITAL
- founded 1668
- for 4 poor women
- moved to The Butts 1765
- now site adjoining Malt Shovel P.H. (called Malt Shovel Cottages)

OLD THWAITES HOSPITAL
- founded 1620
- for 4 poor women
- moved to Hartley Park Avenue 1949
- last part demolished 1960s
- now site of ATS Garage

NEW WARDS HOSPITAL
- moved from Front Street 1932
- for 4 couples/singles
- still in use

Fig. 7 Map showing Pontefract's impressive record of almshouse foundation. *West Yorkshire Archaeology Service.*

Commission which omits many of the smaller almshouses, the total may be close to or indeed exceed that shown in the Directory. Despite changes in nomenclature the almshouse model has continued to be relevant and influential.

Chapter 3

Buildings

Even without a commemorative plaque or inscription, most almshouse buildings are readily recognisable as such. But what are their characteristic features, how were these selected in the first place, and what is implied about the residents and nature of the charity?

A tour of a handful of almshouses in any part of the county soon reveals that there is more than one 'typical' design, and that this does not have a consistent correlation with location, date, size, or even wealth, although all these may contribute. Survival is another factor, and it may be that replacement building, especially in the nineteenth century, has destroyed earlier types without record. Only a few demolished almshouses are illustrated in surviving drawings and photographs. Out of nearly 60 pre-1900 standing buildings listed in the Directory, half a dozen are of seventeenth or late sixteenth century date. Yet these already demonstrate a range of architectural approaches to specific provision for a group of selected elderly poor people within the community. None of these buildings employ the collegiate style and scale found in some southern almshouses and occasionally cited as the norm. Two of the buildings – the earliest ones – are quite exceptional and individual. But behind the intriguing and endearing façade the internal layout shows how the architect/builder addressed the challenges of space and access peculiar to an almshouse and no other kind of building. These two are now discussed in more detail, because although atypical of the almsperson's home during the three centuries, they may offer some guidance on interpreting the buildings, and in their later life indicate some of the change in needs and expectations that affected subsequent design.

The Frieston Hospital [49] was built by the local landowner, Sir John Frieston, in 1595. It was not located on his estates, beside a green or church, nor as part of a philanthropic complex: all possible choices. Instead it was built on a sloping piece of ground, apparently on the edge of the common land or waste which was being rapidly enclosed, and although near to Kirkthorpe church was not associated directly with it. Its siting may reflect an association of ideas. To the north, close to the River Calder (and in a notably damp and waterlogged patch) lay Sagar's Hospital [50] for four women, founded over a generation earlier in 1558. While Sagar's was demolished as unfit in the 1940s, it had been largely rebuilt in the eighteenth century. The accounts (D75/91) for labour and materials (timber, nails, lime and so on) do not record the original layout.

Frieston was designed to accommodate seven 'brothers' or almsmen, one of whom

Fig. 8 Frieston Hospital. a) As seen in 1871 with the top of the massive chimney visible to the left of the roofline. The identifying church should be a little further off. b) Sketch plan showing the communal hall and hearth, access to the brothers' rooms, and the senior brother's room overlooking the entrance. c) Bill itemising labour and materials for repairs to the almshouse and the almswoman's cottage in 1785, paid jointly by Warmfield and Normanton parishes. *W.S. Banks, 1871, Walks about Wakefield (a); author (b); WYAS, W, D75/91 (oblations, parish meetings and constables) (c).*

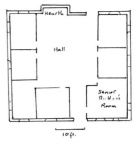

was senior to the rest and given some administrative duties. As these elderly men could not be expected to cope with their own laundry – and possibly cooking, cleaning and a measure of personal hygiene – a woman beneficiary called sister, nurse or matron cared for them. The plan of the building (Fig. 8b) shows how this worked. Six small rooms run along the sides of the building, with a slightly larger one by the entrance. These private rooms open off the communal space which is effectively two storeys in height, lit mainly by the central lantern. The dominant chimneystack is even more apparent inside where the generous hearth has stone benches inset on either side, with rear door and small window adjacent. Outside were privy and fuel store and a separate detached cottage, one-up one-down, within a garden.

When the residents are envisaged, at home in their daily life, they can be seen as part of a micro-community. Each had his own private sleeping space – and it was big enough for a few possessions – while life, at least during the winter, was lived largely in the communal space. Here meals were cooked and eaten, old bones warmed and conversation, if wished, took place. The senior brother (possibly senior in age or the one best fitted to take responsibility as moderately active and not too forgetful) could keep an eye on all comings and goings from his room. He could ensure that no-one was missing untowardly and lock up at night. He also had some responsibility in the distribution of pensions, an aspect discussed in the next chapter. The size and location of his room therefore reflected both function and status.

Meanwhile it was not appropriate for one woman to live in the same house so she was granted the cottage in return for her housekeeping duties. Certainly in later years when personal details were recorded (and passed down as recollections into the last century, Anon. 2000) the 'sister' was herself often elderly and in need of a home; to her the security and useful independence must have been a godsend. Her physical fitness to care for her seven charges was another matter. The garden too is worthy of mention – and this important almshouse feature recurs throughout the survey – as it offered three facilities to the almspeople. A place to sit or maybe stroll outside in good weather was part of a recipe for health and contentment, a plot of land to cultivate avoided the risks of sloth or less worthy occupation, while fruit and vegetables could contribute to the communal economy, either eaten on the premises or sometimes sold (C493/15). Within this useful space the sister had her own garden and no doubt a washing line.

The second of our centripetal almshouses (see Table 2) is considered next to allow for some comparison before the impact of changing ideas may have made such a layout seem irrelevant to the modern life of the seventeenth and eighteenth centuries.

Beamsley Hospital [8] was founded in 1593 by the landowner's wife Margaret Clifford, Countess of Cumberland. It too is centripetal in concept as individual units gather around and are entered from the central common space. The overall shape (Fig. 9a) has produced a segmental room for each of the seven residents. A fireplace makes each room cosy, essential in this high and exposed location, but allows scant space for sitting once a bedstead is installed. The difference lies in the purpose of the communal space. As at Frieston, it is two storeys in height, lit from the lantern roof, but furnished as a small chapel with pews, or perhaps originally simple benches, against the internal walls.

The rooms consist of six of equal size and one larger unit, in this case opposite the doorway, belonging to the 'mother' or matron, who was – at least in theory – elected by the 'sisters' from amongst themselves. How did communal life work here? Cooking, and presumably eating, was individual and relatively private, although with one outer door only all movement, to the pump for water, to the outhouses for fuel or the privy, to enjoy the garden or go on an errand, was equally visible to the other six residents. Here too was a difference as no cleaner/warden/carer was included in the charity, and with no surrounding village and Skipton as market seven miles away, any shopping or social outings must have been restricted. Not everything is recorded, and in practice there must always have been variation between intent and practice and due to individuals involved. Some contact with the wider community was maintained through the visiting reader who conducted services for the residents in their chapel and possibly via the agent for the estates who at a later date liaised both with the reader and the mother over matters of finance and property maintenance (PR/BNA 17/4).

Various suggestions have been put forward (Pacey, Bayer, 2001) to account for Beamsley's unusual design, ranging from the devotional to the occult. However the foundation deed was for a slightly larger establishment, and the second phase which 'more perfectly finished' the almshouses was carried out by Margaret's dutiful daughter Lady Anne Clifford during the 1620s or 1630s to a totally different plan and with no attempt at unification. While the first building lies well back from the busy Skipton – Harrogate road a long path, slightly offcentre, runs down to the newer almshouses and passes through them by an archway to reach the front wall and entrance. The 'new' building is a row of six units, three either side of the archway. They are – or would be but for the sloping terrain – symmetrically spaced. Each is entered by an individual front door, facing away from the road, and comprises a single groundfloor room with fireplace and scullery, the latter probably formed by a later partition. Viewed from outside there would appear to be a first floor but the symmetrical arrangement of windows is deceptive: at one end of the row there is standing height above, at the other only crawling space. No staircase is built in and a reference to wood for ladders (PR/BNA 17/4) has been taken to imply a mezzanine reached by a loft ladder. Effectively these were single room units, but self-contained.

The path joining the two buildings could be a long one in bad weather while the mother in the older building would have no direct view of those living in the lower one. The garden area may have been laid out with tree-lined walks and some seating; there is no mention of cultivation. In the eighteenth century a laundry block was built, demolished after storm damage in the 1960s.

Taken on its own, the second phase at Beamsley sits clearly within the largest category of almshouse plan, that of the row. Long term, and even allowing for nineteenth and twentieth century diversification, this has proved the most popular and enduring form. Lady Anne is known from her diaries and other building projects (Spence, 1997) to have been 'traditional' rather than 'fashionable' and to take a close personal interest in her works, tenants and dependants. Does this change in the early 1600s denote a different attitude to communal living? Did the move towards greater comfort, privacy and separation of activities within the home, apparent in higher status buildings through the period, make an early appearance in accommodation provided for the humble but built to the orders of gentry and aristocracy?

Fig. 9 Beamsley Hospital. a) The earlier building with its single front door, housing six sisters and a mother. The upper window, in the central lantern, admits light to the chapel. b) Gateway through the later row with the family coat of arms above. The sloping ground indicates the change from two storey units to effectively a single storey building. c) The plaque erected by Lady Anne Clifford to mark the completion of the almshouses begun by her mother. d) Sketch plan to indicate the contrast and relationship between the two building phases. *Photos and drawing: author.*

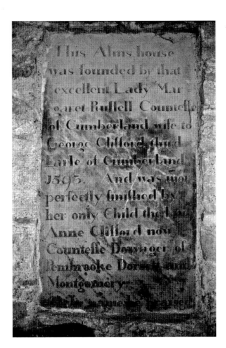

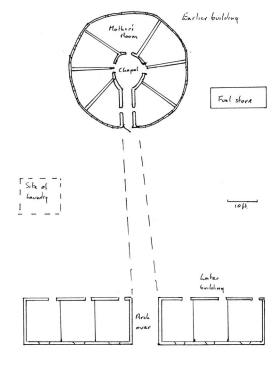

Fig. 10 An excerpt from the Free Press, Saturday 6 November 1895, on the occasion of the Charity Commissioners' enquiry into Frieston Hospital, held by Mr. Wallace. Mr. Whalley was the vicar of Kirkthorpe. An editorial and correspondence followed. *WYAS,W, C547/4/1/5. item 30.*

Mr. Walley proceeded ... ... of the endowments in respect of the Sagar and Freeston Almshouses. In answer to the Inspector, Mr. Walley said the charities had been managed by the Vicar of Kirkthorpe, the Vicar of Normanton, and Mr. Percy Tew, but latterly the Charity Commissioners had refused to recognise these three, and insisted on the signatures being obtained of the original five Vicars who, failing the appointment of other trustees, were to be the trustees of the Hospital, viz., the Vicars of Warmfield, Normanton, Pontefract, Leeds, and Wakefield. The yearly income at present from all sources was approximately £115 8s. 8d. Last year they received £383 19s. 1d., including £250 obtained especially for rebuilding and alterations. At present there were three pensioners in the Freeston Hospital, only one of whom, however, was in residence, the other two being ill and with friends. Originally there was accommodation for seven pensioners and a matron, but three of the rooms had been made into one, which was now used as a parish room, and on Sundays for a Sunday school.—Mr. Wallace: Is it open for everyone in the parish?—Mr. Walley: No.—Mr. Wallace: The Church only?—Mr. Walley: No, the Parish Council meet here, and there have also been parish meetings. The Parish Council have agreed to pay 2s. 6d. for each meeting to the trustees.—Mr. Austwick said the Sunday School ought to pay rent also—in fact he thought it was not right to annoy the old people who lived there by the holding of a Sunday School in the building.—In answer to Mr. Wallace, the Vicar said there was practically no other place where a Sunday School could be held—the Heath School was too far. Mr. Walley added that Mr. Skirrow, who conducted the last inquiry, had said it was a gross perversion of trust, but although it had been said that the old men were annoyed by the children, the fact was that they were annoyed at being obliged to live there at all.—Mr. Muirhead said they were much better off there than at the Workhouse.—Mr. Wallace: Do you think it would be better to give pensions?—The Vicar said he was not prepared to answer that question. The trustees had at present under their consideration a proposed new scheme, but they had not yet come to any decision.—Mr. Wallace asked what was paid at present.—Mr. Walley said each pensioner was paid 6s. a week whether he lived there or not, but the trustees insisted upon residence, except where it was absolutely necessary for the men to be away, in which case a medical certificate was insisted upon. They also gave each pensioner a load of coal a year. The Sagar's hospital was in a very low position, and really in an uninhabitable state, and as the architect stated that the renovation would cost almost as much as rebuilding, the trustees proposed to rebuild on the land above the Freeston Hospital.—Mr. Thompson said the Sagar's charity was left for four poor people of the parish. Should they be entitled to send a pensioner from Sharlston?—Mr. Wallace said he thought so.

Later history of both Frieston and Beamsley shows a distinct decline in popularity, that is, in applications for residence, in the later nineteenth and early twentieth century. There could be an array of causes for this, peculiar to each case. At Frieston, social changes within the wider community as well as insensitive use of parts of the building for other communal purposes (Sunday school and parish meetings) were certainly factors, although feelings of 'ownership' and responsibility indicate the continuing relevance to the wider community (C 547). In Beamsley the situation appears to have been more straightforward. A relatively isolated situation and lack of modern facilities, despite successive renovations, resulted in a number of non-resident almswomen. That is to say, they accepted their place and collected their pension from the charity but failed to occupy the premises as expected by the terms of the foundation (CC, ii, 763). Certainly some almshouses were 'lost' due to conversion of their charity to the provision of out-pensions only, but where this was contrary to the founder's intentions it could not be done legally on an ad hoc basis.

The buildings at Frieston and Beamsley remained structurally sound. It is perhaps significant that they survive, externally unaltered, but no longer almshouses or in any form of multiple occupation or communal use. One is a private family house, the other let as holiday accommodation. Choices in regard to privacy and communality may properly be a matter for the individual, but it may be noted that fashions within twentieth century 'old people's homes', sheltered housing and 'care in the community' were driven by the providers not the residents or recipients. Although some shared facilities were incorporated in almshouse design through the intervening period, for the most part this was overtaken by independence and the sense of respect this confers.

Table 2 Building layout, for extant almshouse buildings (including rebuilds)

Row	Courtyard	Centripetal	Semi-detached
39	13	2	5

Choice of layout: the row

The most numerous and enduring form, throughout the period, is the row. Typically, although not universally, this is a single storey row of half a dozen units, each with a separate entrance and tall chimney stack. A plaque gives the founder's name and date and may form part of a central feature. As half the surviving almshouses and possibly even more of those replaced evince these characteristics it is worth considering both the structural features and their implications in more detail.

At the risk of stating the obvious, it might be said that a row or terrace is one of the commonest forms of construction, especially where accommodation is to be provided for a number of households at one build. Structurally, it offers economy of materials as well as ground space, with shared or grouped utilities and overall stability. Comparisons are readily made with mill-workers' terraces and perhaps more appositely with planned villages and estate housing. Fewer single storey homes of agricultural labourers or their urban counterparts survive although looking outside the county Scotland and Ireland offer numerous examples. Ironically, the single storey dwelling regarded as inadequate in space and facilities, and often of cheap materials or poorly maintained, was reinvented as the twentieth century bungalow. Despite the colonial image the form has been – and still is – often targeted towards older and less active residents in single or two-person households. The chimneys which catch the eye as disproportionately tall (giving a good draw to the fire) are the least stable element and most likely to have been rebuilt.

While this explains some of the practical attractions of the form, the aesthetic and emotional impact on the onlooker is one of order, neatness and symmetry. Three examples show how this is achieved: Mary Lowther's Hospital at Ackworth [2] built in 1741, Joseph Smith's Almshouses at Thornton–in–Craven [100] erected 1815, and Robert Nettleton's Almshouses at Almondbury [3] rebuilt in 1863.

At Ackworth (Fig. 1) each of the six units has an identical pattern of front door and window, three placed either side of a central, more formal element where a Classical pediment above the Gibbs door surround breaks the skyline and unifies the whole. The pediment accommodates the foundation plaque while at the rear the central unit is found to extend into the enclosed garden. This was the home of the schoolmaster and his family. Mary Lowther wished to support youthful and elderly vulnerable members of the community but that alone would not explain the architectural relationship. Rather it reflects social structure in miniature: the professional or official of higher status is not separated from the rest but has a responsible role (care and control in undefined proportion) towards the other beneficiaries of the charity. Hierarchy is stated architecturally as the social order is affirmed.

Symmetry is a slightly different issue, though not necessarily so perceived or articulated at the time of building. At Thornton–in–Craven (Fig. 11) as a reminder that all classification produces exceptions and grey areas, the superficially similar single storey row of local stone with its stone slate roof and central Classical pediment was designed for five almswomen. While the ground plan shows greater generosity of space –two rooms rather than one – a communal kitchen was originally provided. Was this a late physical survival of the communal ideal or was it due to individual instructions from Rachel Smith who established the almshouses on her late husband's behalf? There is no record of how the kitchen was utilised on a day-to-day basis. The façade does not acknowledge the function but displays satisfying architectural symmetry. The sense of regularity may be indicative of well-ordered lives.

Fig. 11 Joseph Smith's Almshouses. Part of the stone row with its Classical pediment. *Photo: author.*

Fig. 12 Hannah Rawson's Almshouses. The protruding end gable allows the rooms in this unit to be placed at right angles to the main body of the row. *Photo: author.*

Other examples of rows could be cited, for instance in Bradford at the Melbourne Almshouses [11] and Ripley (Bowling Dye Works) Almshouses, where the terminal units in each case present a gable to the front. This approach gives variety whilst achieving not only symmetry but containment, a statement of unification and definition of the bounds of that particular small community. In order that each resident should have parity of space end gables might be brought forward, as may be seen at Wadsley [104], so that a two-room unit has one room behind the other instead of side by side. The essential row can thus develop wings, as will be seen shortly.

To return to the simpler form, Almondbury, while graced with a lengthy inscription due to the need to do justice to all involved in the rebuild, is otherwise unadorned: no pediment, central feature or decorative gables or barge boards. Here choice of materials and scale are the distinctive features. Employment of pediments and gables may reflect contemporary fashion – Classical, Gothic or more eclectic indulgence – but choice of material and quality of workmanship place almshouses in an interesting and possibly individual category. They are neither strictly polite nor vernacular, although examples may be found towards both ends of the spectrum. Almost always materials (excluding later repairs) are those found locally: stone or brick according to place and time. Features such as graduated stone slates (see Figs. 73 and 78) reflect local practice. Opportunities for something a little above the basic lie in the door and window surrounds as in the

Fig. 13 The simple unadorned row of six almshouses at Almondbury, rebuilt in 1863 by the trustees of Robert Nettleton's Charity. *Photo: author.*

long and short work and three-light mullions at Almondbury, or in stone detailing on a brick building, inessential hood moulds or string course on a two-storey building.

Finance must have been a consideration in determining design and finish, and with a fixed sum of money and predetermined number of units to be built, may not have offered much leeway. Very little (see Chapter Four) is recorded in the way of detailed architectural specifications by almshouse founders. Respectability, permanence (reflecting an endowed charity as much as anticipation of need) and status (of all concerned) were surely elements. More complex messages about the rewards of virtue and obedience or social conformity, moral status, independence and regulation, may well be implicit, but how these were interpreted by neighbours, residents and outsiders remains unknown. In many cases, decisions within the understood 'almshouse model' may have fallen largely to the builder or echo imprecisely what had been seen elsewhere.

Occasionally almshouses – or to be precise the façade and any other parts accessed by those other than the residents, their friends and helpers – were promoted beyond their station in life to join the imposing and architect-designed. In the case of Fountain's Hospital at Linton [62] built 1721, and the Gascoigne Almshouses at Aberford [1] founded in 1844, both rows in essential plan, the effect is not so much imposing as overwhelming: Classical and Gothic examples of the wow factor in unexpected locations. It could be claimed that the exceptional merit less attention (and should be

Fig. 14 Gascoigne Almshouses. Lithograph engraved by A. Maclure, published by Maclure, Macdonald and Macgregor, Leeds and Liverpool, c. 1845. Visitors, probably including the founding sisters, feature more prominently than almspeople, of whom there were eight. *Leeds Museums and Galleries (Lotherton Hall).*

put firmly in their place) than the generality. But in each case here something is known of the founder in connection with the end product. Richard Fountain supplied timber to Vanbrugh, whose style the Hospital closely imitates (Pevsner, 1967, 353), while the artistic Gascoigne sisters were involved in ecclesiastical design and possibly glasswork (White, 2004). These concerns of the founders are more apparent than the needs of the poor, to the extent that the Charity Commissioners were led to comment on the expenditure on building (£40,000) at Aberford in relation to the eight beneficiaries (CC, iv, 9). At Linton, tower, cupola and Venetian window do not immediately speak of charity until the characteristic grouping of doors is noted on the façade and inturned wings, while the entire edifice seems too large for its location, hemmed in by cottages on one side and the stream on the other. Even the green does not offer enough space for the prospect that seems to be intended.

By way of contrast, Stapleton Cottages or Carlton Almshouses [16] at Carlton near Goole are among the least ostentatious. The short row of four (with another cottage abutting one end) was rebuilt in 1901 of local red brick and pantiles. Apart from the plaque enumerating members of the Beaumont family responsible for the rebuild, there is nothing to suggest status or function other than that of farm labourers' or humble estate workers' homes. Indeed there is less presence than that seen in the estate houses of 1877 on the main street. Location and alignment may reflect an earlier village layout but perhaps the very simplicity placed the retired residents on a level with those still working as these almshouses remained, and to some extent still do, in the gift of the landowner.

An almshouse of fewer than four units is rare and hardly fits the description of a row. Prospective benefactors unable to fund large building projects might prefer to make additions to existing charities, as happened at Mary Potter's Almshouse in Leeds

Fig. 16 Carlton Almshouses. The simplicity of design in local brick and pantiles suggests cottages for farm labourers or other estate workers. These houses are still essentially single room bedsits with a rear lean-to. *Photo: author.*

[59] founded in 1728 and attracting at least three further donations which allowed expansion. However a few instances are recorded of existing cottages being used as almshouses (see Holroyd's Almshouses [46]). The smallest extant almshouse, in terms of the number of units, is at Flockton [32] where a pair of cottages, Carter's Almshouses, was rebuilt in 1868. In local brick and slate, the building is dignified by stone quoins and decorative bargeboards with a plaque noting the original foundation of 1697 on the gable end, presumably to be viewed from the adjoining churchyard rather than the access lane. Internally the units of one room plus lean-to are no smaller than those found in larger groupings. It is sad to see this building empty and in a state of decay.

A few other instances of pairs of units date entirely to the nineteenth century, although there were earlier two-unit almshouses in Pontefract before amalgamation and rebuilding. The Victorian examples have a semi-detached air: Harrison's Homes at Pledwick [68]1885, Eleanor Hirst's small two-storey 'villas' at Wilshaw [114] 1871 and the upmarket John Abbott's Trustees Ladies' Homes [35] built in their private park in Halifax in 1886. Tables 2 and 3 give a breakdown of the surviving almshouse buildings by form and style.

Fig. 17 Carter's Almshouses. Romantic ruin or sad dereliction: an uninhabited pair of almshouses, with the decorative bargeboards framing the foundation plaque. *Photo: author.*

Fig. 18 Semi-detached pairs of almshouses: a) Harrison's Homes for the Aged Poor: two of the three commodious semis designed by Frederick Simpson who was also responsible for the former Marsland's Almshouses in Wakefield; b) one of the three pairs of Eleanor Hirst's Almshouses at Wilshaw. *Photos: author.*

Table 3 Architectural style, for extant almshouse buildings (including rebuilds)

Classical	Gothic	Unadorned	Eclectic
6	20	26	7

NB. Classification is not always clearcut as elements of more than one characteristic may be found together.

Table 4 Size of charity: numbers of beneficiaries (excluding later changes)

Small 2–6	Medium 7–13	Large 14+	Uncertain
67	32	14	2

The courtyard form

Beyond the rare centripetal, occasional pairs and ubiquitous rows already discussed, the other form is the courtyard. This category includes both enclosed models with gated access to the centre and all the units facing inwards and regular or irregular three-sided groupings with the contained quadrangle or garden an important feature. This strand in the received available forms for an almshouse is to be found chronologically alongside

Fig. 19 The symmetrical layout of Bryan Cooke's almshouses seen from the entrance to the courtyard. *Photo: author.*

the row, including Arksey [5] built in 1660 and the Bradford Tradesmens' Home [14] of 1875. Examples may be single storey and unadorned as in the former or two storey with decorative dormers and finials as at the latter (Fig. 20). In Halifax, brothers and business partners Frank and Joseph Crossley each established substantial almshouse charities [36, 37]: Frank favoured a row while Joseph and his son Edward developed a courtyard layout. At Waddington [103] where older buildings were replaced in 1893 by a courtyard plan, illustrations show an earlier row or rows (Fig. 86). Indeed, there seems to have been a rise in popularity of the courtyard form from the mid-nineteenth century, especially for larger foundations. The extensive archive covering the rebuilding

Fig. 20 An engraving of the large scale open courtyard form at Bradford Tradesmens' Home, with the chapel centre right and the secretary's house on the left of the picture. *Bradford Tradesmens' Home Trustees.*

Fig. 21 Archbishop Holgate's Hospital. Detail from the architect's presentation drawing (unsigned) showing the distinctive banded brickwork and bays, also proposed side ranges which were never built. *Trustee Collection.*

of Archbishop Holgate's Hospital [41] at Hemsworth in 1858 suggests a preference for the courtyard layout and a possible intention that the two long rows in parallel on the spacious site might later be connected by two side ranges (TC).

What was the thinking behind these choices? Factors may have been as much pragmatic and functional as symbolic or theoretical. Without statements of intent by founders or builders our interpretation of their motives remains speculative, informed by hints from their life and work, connections and resources.

The courtyard form does satisfy some practical requirements, notably in accommodating larger groups of 20 or more upon a plot of ground in a more sociable and visually satisfying way than is achieved by setting out a long row or pair of rows as happened at Bentham [9] although this naturally depends on the land available. It can offer more equality of access in the sense of individual units' distance from the outer world and also from the grouped or shared facilities of fuel stores, privies and in some places, wash house, than is present in a row at right-angles to the frontage or a long row without through passage or individual back doors.

But shape of plot and number of units were not the sole factors. The courtyard form offered communal space, at least a feeling of enhanced security and gave the residents a measure of privacy (if not from each other) whilst allowing the founder scope for a suitable statement of beneficence. Within the enclosed space almspeople might stroll or sit in peace and comfort, whether the area was cobbled or planted. Until the later nineteenth century they would probably fetch water from the communal pump situated here, as may still be seen at the Audus and Feoffee Square Almshouses in Selby [87]. Little is known of the original appearance of courtyards and possibly this depended

Fig. 22 Harrison's Hospital, Leeds. The photograph was taken within the paved courtyard in 1925. The archway on the right leads to the churchyard; the former water pump is in the centre. *Leeds Library and Information Service, 200275–47948855.*

on individual residents, some being compulsive gardeners and others prone to dump surplus items outdoors! Present day almshouse courtyards range in style from the Mediterranean image of containers at Carleton-in-Craven [15] to the massed rose beds of Bradford Tradesmens' Home [14]. Listed buildings' regulations do not extend to the grounds.

The almshouses at Wentworth [111] founded in 1697 illustrate some of the diversity and restrictions of the form (Fig. 23). The front façade is two storey, with entry through a gated central arch beneath a clock tower: effectively the row with central feature, itself reached by a gated path through the narrow garden. Within the enclosed area the other three ranges are found to be single storey, facing inwards with individual front doors, the rear range pierced by a through passage. Recent alterations include the insertion of back doors, a feature noticeably lacking elsewhere; if the outer gate to the courtyard was not merely closed but locked, this would control the residents' movements. The issue of a curfew is discussed in the next chapter.

Overall the impression is of a contained, orderly and inward-looking but not closed small community. If a model is sought for this image the most likely one is that of the pre-Reformation religious house and the collegiate way of life. The popularity of this approach in the second half of the nineteenth century would seem to reflect the spirit of romantic medievalism, a folk memory (for those who could afford it) recreated by Pugin (1836) and illustrated in a series of historical notes in *The Builder* (1847–67).

Indoors

Meanwhile the almshouse residents were more likely to be concerned with the interior of their homes. In the first place, how much living space was seen as appropriate? The majority of units were intended as single person bedsits, planned for one elderly person whether widowed or single. Some, generally later, charities included suitable elderly couples within their remit, and in a very few places (for instance, Joseph Crossley's Almshouses [37]) units were built to different sizes. On the other hand a few, mostly

Fig. 23 Aspects of Wentworth Hospital: a) the entrance through the secluded garden and gateway; b) the courtyard of single storey brick ranges with the disused well beneath the crossing of the paths; c) a back view of the south range showing its junction with the taller, more stately street range. The back doors were provided in the twentieth century. *Photos: author.*

earlier, charities expected residents to share in pairs. Whenever possible, this idea was abandoned, even at a loss in the number of potential beneficiaries. The Charity Commissioners observed the problem on their visit to Harrison's Hospital in Leeds [55]. Sharing was 'productive of great inconvenience as it prevented those who became feeble and bedridden from having any friend or relative attend them' while 'by differences of temper and other causes quarrels were of constant occurrence', some not on speaking terms, even chalking a line across the floor (CC, iv, 368). New buildings dealt with the problem here, while the mention of carers should be noted, to be followed up in the next chapter.

The basic unit has been described here as a bedsit to indicate a general purpose room for living and sleeping, with the more sophisticated examples incorporating a bed alcove (see Figs. 25, 26, 58 and 59 for plans). The fireplace was an essential feature for heating, cooking and heating water, while to the rear of the room there might be a small outshut or pantry. Style and furnishing of the living space, where most hours were passed by the almsperson, are the aspects about which we know least. Where historic building legislation and local pride in their charity have preserved the parts of the building visible to the onlooker, internal modernisation has often been extensive, commonly with rear extensions to accommodate bathroom and kitchen, and in some cases redivision of the internal space. An alternative conversion has been a reduction in

Fig. 24 Galleries providing access: a) at Spence's Hospital, Carleton-in-Craven, where the wide central door formerly led to the communal area; b) the largely unadorned Cotton Horne's Almshouses in Wakefield with porches on both levels for access to the units on either side. *Photos: author.*

the number of units by joining two internally (apparent from the numbering on front doors) hence creating apartments in place of bedsits.

Some almshouses were built as two-room units, allowing the superior convenience of a separate sleeping area, also with the attached pantry or scullery. The second room might be alongside, although fenestration suggests that this was uncommon, behind and sometimes under the slope of the roof, or, of course, upstairs in a two storey house. Single storey buildings outnumber the others two to one, while the second floor may contain separate units, accessed by a gallery, as at Spence's Hospital [15] built in 1698 and the much later Cotton Horne's Almshouses [107] rebuilt in 1901. The way in which stairs fitted into the one-up, one-down houses may be seen in the architects' drawings for Joseph Crossley's Almshouses [37] and for Holroyd's Almshouses in Huddersfield [46] prior to modernisation (Figs. 25a and b). In most cases the upper room was left open to the roof. The relative merits of storage space and greater headroom may be weighed against heat loss and drafts. In a few instances, cellars were built, but found to be hazardous (pers. com.). In some places too the second room was little used due to damp and lack of ventilation. Damp, as the Charity Commissioners observed, was also found where stone floors were laid directly on the ground, a problem encountered by many householders. These are negative points, but in the overwhelming majority of cases, buildings were solid, and must often have exceeded the quality of the almsperson's original home, whether urban or rural. The key in either case was maintenance, dependent on the will and resources of the landlord, in this case the charity's trustees.

A person in need of an almshouse charity might reasonably be expected to have few possessions – memories rather than mementoes – and indeed might need assistance with basic effects. Dimensions for the living or only room ranged from 12 x 12 ft (360 x 360 cm) to 16 x 14 ft 6 in (480 x 435 cm). Perkins and Sons' plans for St. Anne's Hospital in Ripon [80] rebuilt in 1869, show single rooms of 13 x 12 ft 6 in (390 x 375 cm) internally, with a bed alcove behind an inset porch, pantry opening onto a rear scullery and toilet, with fireplace and cupboard neatly included. This compact dwelling is unusual only in being designed as two rows of four, back-to-back (Fig. 26).

Within the total space available, allowing for the hearth, opening doors and some room to move about, one would expect to find a bed, chair, table and probably second chair, as well as a chest or cupboard and hooks to keep clothes and utensils. Records are tantalising and no illustrations have been found. Mr. Armstrong, the Master at Archbishop Holgate's Hospital at Hemsworth [41] was instructed by the trustees as the rebuild neared completion to 'furnish one of the empty houses in such manner as he thinks every house ought to be fitted up, viz. the bedroom with an iron bedstead, a row of pegs and a receptacle of some kind for linen and cloths. The sitting room with a delf-case [dresser], blinds and rollers and the kitchen with a towel roller and shelves – such articles to be deemed permanent fixtures' (C 345/1). Alas, no description or separate accounts are given of the items duly installed. It seems probable that the bedstead as the heaviest and least manoeuvrable item was often provided by the charity, and this might be sensible in terms of hygiene. It is also probable that some charities, or the trustees as individuals, assisted in providing furniture, although this level of detail seldom reaches their minute books. Furniture must also have been left from one occupant to the next and if still usable would have had no other ready 'home'. But sometimes even the bare

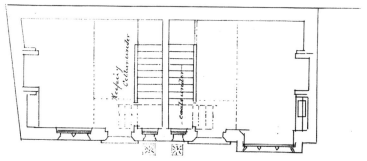

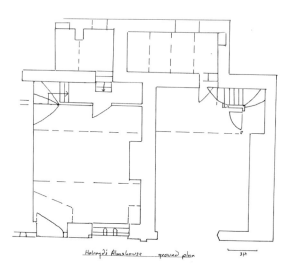

Fig. 25 Internal arrangements for two storey homes: a) architect's drawing, also showing cellars, at Joseph Crossley's Almshouses in Halifax; b) detail of Holroyd's Almshouse, Huddersfield, drawn by Charles Horsfall, architects, prior to modernisation. *Trustee collection (a); WYAS,K KC627 3/1 (b).*

Fig. 26 St. Anne's Hospital (Maison de Dieu), Ripon. a) The plans produced by the architects Perkin and Son of Leeds for the 1869 rebuilding show a back-to-back layout giving garden views to all residents, although space would seem to have been sufficient to allow two rows or a small courtyard. No visual connection is made with the ruin of the ancient chapel by the roadside. b) The layout, as built, provided a living room (labelled kitchen) with a bed recess for sleeping and the scullery for washing and preparing meals. The compact design is apparent in the section and elevation which show scullery windows at one end of the row only; no information is given on drainage. *North Yorkshire County Record Office, DC/RIC, ix 2/5/9 and 2/5/10.*

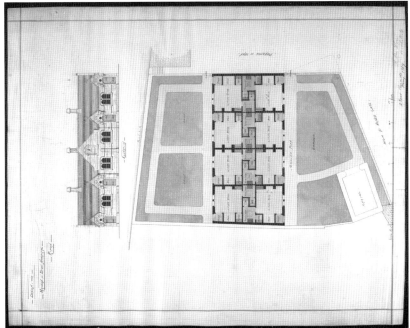

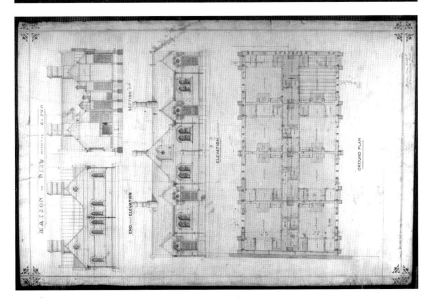

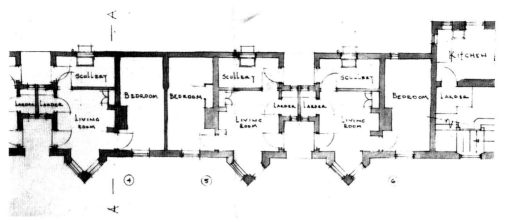

Fig. 27 Archbishop Holgate's Hospital. Detail from an architect's plan (drawn after 1914 and before the 1950s modifications) showing the internal layout comprising three rooms and a bay to each unit. *Trustee Collection.*

essentials would have fitted awkwardly in the space available. Consider making the bed in the segmental chambers at Beamsley or lighting a fire in the bedroom at Hemsworth (see Figs. 9 and 27).

Outdoors

External space was often more generous and both the immediate surroundings and the location were important factors in siting almshouses. They need to be understood as part of the concept even where later changes have taken place. In the case of a row of almshouses a strip of front garden is generally found, often with individual gates and paths to each door, and a common path – which may be wide enough for a bench – running along the front of the building. To the rear a larger common space is most often found, including a lawn and drying ground and sometimes an additional paved area. The grounds are enclosed by a wall of sufficient height to grant privacy, deter intruders and clearly define the boundaries of the property. The frequency of the model suggests the layout is original, modernised only by the removal of redundant outbuildings.

Less certain and perhaps less consistent is the extent of a resident's right and responsibility for an individual area of garden. Waterhouse Smith specified in 1839 that his almspeople at Cawood [18] should care for their gardens which must 'be distinguished by great neatness and nice order' (CC, v, 122). Certainly today they present a colourful and varied display, whilst the charity maintains the rear lawn and borders. Charities prosperous enough to employ staff might include a gardener, permanently as at Bradford Tradesmens' Home [14] or on a casual basis as at Joseph Crossley's Almshouses [37]. Beyond the decorative, a garden offered the opportunity to cultivate fruit and vegetables, and this productive aspect may have been as much part of some founders' intentions as a green and healthy space and discreet laundry area. At the Gascoigne Almshouses at Aberford [1] the almsmen were expected to care for the extensive grounds and grow produce as some return for their gracious accommodation. Residents of the other almshouses in Cawood, James's Hospital [17] had their individual gooseberry gardens (CC, v, 117). But while the cottage garden (or later, the allotment)

Fig. 28 Gardens: a) stepped front garden at Leathley; b) avenue leading to the gatehouse at Hemsworth; c) J.W. Petty's plan of 1880 for grounds to complement Joseph Crossley's Almshouses. *Photos: author (a and b); Trustee Collection (c).*

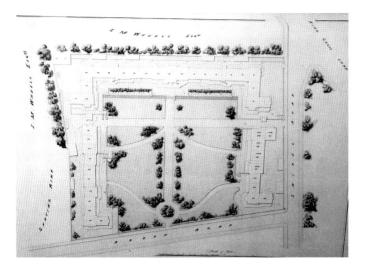

might be the social model, how many almspeople had the inclination or energy for digging and weeding? It is known that residents at Spence's Hospital [15] were unable to maintain the grounds, which were taken on by more active neighbours (pers. com.).

Beyond the garden and their own enclave, almspeople might encounter various

Fig. 29 A gathering of almshouses at Almondbury: a) from right to left, Robert Nettleton's, Emily Parkin's and Houghton's; b) continuity of character shown in Emily Parkin's 1931 building. *Photos: author.*

surroundings. Despite considerations of quiet and security, location was often central, giving residents a place within the community, access to amenities and a prospect of local life from which they were not excluded. It should also be said that such a site enabled the generosity of the founder to be kept in full view. Again little has been recorded of motives in selecting a site, except when a rebuild has involved nineteenth-century trustees in the acquisition of land. Practical considerations included an adequate water supply (condemned in a number of cases by Sanitary Inspectors as environmental health standards rose) and healthy high ground, above marsh or urban pollution. Avoidance of flooding was at issue when the Earl of Shrewsbury's Hospital in Sheffield [93] left its riverside location in 1768 after four fatalities; the new site faced the typhoid monument. Holmfirth Monumental Almshouses [42] erected as a result of a public appeal after the Bilberry Reservoir disaster were located high up on the outskirts of the town.

A site given free of charge was an obvious attraction, and the trustees of Robert Nettleton's Almshouses at Almondbury [3] were delighted with the gift of land from

Sir John Ramsden. This also had the advantage of being centrally located within the catchment area of a scattered and hilly parish, as the trustees' deliberations prior to the rebuild had focused on the importance of residents' nearness to friends and familiar places. Almondbury also shows the effect of attraction as two later groups of almshouses joined the cluster: Emily Parkin's in 1931 and more recently Houghton's.

On the other hand, a central location in an urban context has accounted for a number of twentieth-century demolitions. Town planning and changing ideas on suitable housing for the elderly led the demands of road-widening to affect William Horne's Almshouse at Mexborough [65] as early as 1910, while the expansion of shopping centres caused Harrison's Hospital [55] to leave what had been a green field site in seventeenth-century Leeds. Sale of such prime sites enabled astute trustees to rebuild and update their provision; while historic buildings were regrettably lost without any adequate recording, the objects of some of these charities prospered.

Statement of identity

The sole fragment liable for preservation in these circumstances is the foundation plaque. Plaques, symbols or quotations appear on the majority of almshouse buildings, ranging from the basic to the ostentatious. They may serve as little more than the address or give more detail about the founder and purpose of the charity. Most often the plaque

Fig. 30 The Hospital Houses at Mexborough. The photograph (a) suggests the old two storey row may have suffered from subsidence prior to demolition in 1910. The replacement row (b) used a pair of protruding gables to accommodate coats of arms and inscriptions over four of the six doors. The design recalls that of Mary Bellamy's at Rotherham. *Doncaster Archive, D2. MD 542/1 nos. 12 and 14.*

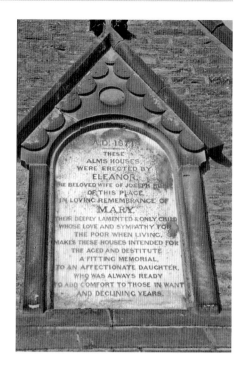

Fig. 31 Acknowledgements to founders and donors: a) one of the pair of plaques displayed on the gables of the Ripley Almshouses at Bradford, built by a local employer who also provided some model housing and the nearby park; b) the inscription at Wilshaw commemorating the founder's daughter who predeceased her parents; c) obelisk erected by the Licensed Victuallers Association in Sheffield; d) coat of arms and texts adorning the central tower of Frank Crossley's Almshouses in Halifax. *Photos: author.*

is located centrally, over a front door, as part of a central feature, or on an entrance arch or gateway. At Ripley Almshouses [13] foundation and rebuilding are commemorated symmetrically on the two terminal gables while the almshouse at Crigglestone [19] is identified under both old and new names, Worrill's and Victoria Memorial. A lengthy notice incorporating later bequests at Spence's Hospital [15] does not occupy a central position, but one where it is more visible to outsiders, likewise Leathley, Bentham and Long Preston have plaques less aesthetically placed on the gable end for the convenience of road access. In Sheffield, the Licensed Victuallers Association [92] chose to display their inscription on a small obelisk in the grounds, acknowledging financial assistance received following 'the spirited example' of their first donor.

The simplest format gives name and date, for instance 'Holroyd's Almshouse 1830', which may be elaborated to give additional family members a share of the glory as in Leeds [61] 'These almshouses were erected by Martha Walker Nancroft House Armley in memory of her parents brothers and sister AD 1883'. Martha would appear to be the last member of her family. Sometimes a husband is named by the widow, or brother by his surviving sister, as in the case of Henry and Ann Hitch at Leathley [52] while at Wilshaw [114] the daughter is commemorated by her grieving mother. These almshouses are thus memorials to the deceased as well as to the kindly intentions of the founder. In line with the current custom of providing named seats in public parks, the individual's name is kept in daily view with happy associations. Perhaps emotionally this could be claimed as the last link with the medieval chantries mentioned in Chapter Two.

Some plaques give more information on the nature and scope of the charity as in the statement at Ackworth [2] 'Mary Lowther erected and endowed this hospital for a schoolmaster and six poor women 1741'. Bryan Cooke's weatherworn plaque at Arksey [5] followed by that of the great-nephew responsible for repairs is unusual in giving details of selection criteria and pensions in Latin. Explanatory plaques that accompany rebuilding may take on the style of civic foundation stones, listing all dignitaries involved, although the inscription at Horbury [44] which names the Queen and the bishop fails to explain the transition from Wormald's to St. Leonard's Hospital. Founders may be named more subtly, especially on Victorian Gothic buildings, by incorporating initials into the decorative scheme as at Joseph Crossley's Almshouses [37]. Coats of arms may have a similar function. Beamsley [8] proudly displays the arms of Countess Margaret and her husband on the later building erected by their daughter. The unpretentious Melbourne Almshouses [11] have an unexpected shield and crest, but too weatherworn to be informative.

A brief Biblical quotation might also serve to reinforce the dual message of the building's function and the founder's godly nature. Frank Crossley placed date and initials on the end towers of his almshouse [36] and coat of arms (he was knighted as Sir Francis) and scroll centrally: 'of thine own have we given thee'. Sir John Frieston [49] reminds us that 'He that hath mercy on the poor, happy is he' – and one must hope that this was so, though doubtless the intention was to encourage others to do likewise. At Wadsley [104] Hannah Rawson chose the wording 'thus said the Lord "and even to your old age I am He"'. Residents and neighbours of Lydia Freeman's Hospital near Sheffield [90] may have been cheered by the motto displayed between the crenellations and the entrance to the reading room, 'Dum Spiro Spero' ('while there's life there's hope').

Finally, a more sculptural form of commemoration should be mentioned, although examples are now lacking in the county. This would be either a statue or bust of the founder or almsperson. The committee appointed by Pontefract town council in 1854 to report on their 'almshouses and miscellaneous charities' observed at Frank's Hospital [71] 'a rude and much defaced representation of a bedesman' (Jefferson, 1854). One of the latest foundations of the period, Scott's in Leeds [60] displays a posthumous example of a founder's bust, while Joseph Crossley is similarly commemorated in the chapel of his almshouses [37]. Symbolic of the background of founder and beneficiaries were the beehive at Rogers' Almshouse [40] for hard-working tradespeople, and the stone alpaca (originally in Titus Salt's garden) beside the Bradford Tradesmens' chapel [14] as a reminder of the woollen trade.

But for the most part the buildings themselves, style, substance and location, make sufficient statements. The act of philanthropy lives on in its daily implementation.

Fig. 32 Commemoration in stone: a) the founder's bust, erected posthumously, at John Scott's Almshouses in Leeds; b) bust of Joseph Crossley displayed in a niche behind the altar in the almshouse chapel; c) details of the beehive motif and inscription over the door to the tower at Rogers' Almshouses in Harrogate. *Photos: author.*

Chapter 4

People

The man or woman who entered or 'was admitted' to an almshouse was elderly and poor and able to demonstrate those conditions. The terms of the foundation, often set out in the founder's will or in a constitution (discussed later in this chapter) might be no more specific than this. The essential element was that the potential almsperson was no longer able to support him or herself by employment and so age might be paralleled by infirmity.

Who might be eligible?

If demand exceeded supply, priorities were needed. Seniority might secure a place, as at Arksey [5] designated for the '12 paupertate et senio maximi laborantium' (12 oldest and poorest working people), while Wentworth [111] was similarly intended for 'the ancientest and poorest inhabitants'. Is this a simple assumption of needs increasing with age, an easy criterion to assess, or an indication of respect accorded the achievement and status of advanced age? From the eighteenth century onwards a minimum age was usually set, most commonly 60–65, but sometimes less, as low as 40 at Ackworth [2]. There might be some discretion on health grounds and Joseph Crossley [36] ensured that future appropriate applicants should not be turned down by too rigid a reading of the rules. Clause 13 set a minimum age of 70, but allowed younger applicants, over 60, if 'incapacitated for labour either by disease or infirmity' (CC, iii, 120).

A minimum age of 60–65 may look like modern society's concept of retirement, but it should be remembered that life expectancy was considerably lower and particularly among industrial workers. 'Retirement' was not accompanied by any form of state support, while most homes were rented. Inability to work meant inability to pay the rent; the elderly person left in the family home, without savings, was most likely to move in with the younger generation (or vice versa). Where there was no available family network – no children or none surviving, family moved away, emigrated or lost touch, or relatives themselves living in poverty with inadequate resources – then the almshouse was an attractive option. The ability or otherwise of relatives to care for the elderly could be open to interpretation and minute books hint at some of the struggles that must have ensued, with duty ranged beside 'care in the community'.

Inability to work, or do sufficient to support oneself, for medical reasons could be due to occupational disease. Booth noted in Sheffield in 1893 that men suffered and were often 'killed off by the heavy character of iron and steel works, grinders' disease, lead colic, phthisis and intemperance' (Booth, 1894, no. 55) while agricultural workers were subject to farmer's lung, arthritis and rheumatism, exacerbated by damp living as well as working conditions. Almswomen might suffer from failing eyesight which prevented earnings from sewing. Elizabeth Barlow, who applied to the almshouse at Hemsworth in 1900 had 'of late years supported herself by needlework' but could no longer manage and 'now aged 69 also suffered from rheumatism and a weak heart' (C 345/1/20). Almswomen were often widows whose main source of income had ceased on the death of the spouse.

The issue of health will be mentioned again later, but – as there are always some exceptions to the generality – it should be said that in a very few almshouses some work was expected in return. This could be in the form of upkeep of the premises – and almspeople were always expected to keep their own homes clean – or as a contribution towards the communal life style. This was the case at Aberford [1] from the 1840s where the almswomen were required to clean and wash for all the residents, while the men cultivated the grounds, yet a maid was employed and dinners provided.

While this certainly was unusual it is worth remembering too that rules and intentions were not necessarily the same as feasibility and implementation.

After age and means, the most commonly stated criteria were gender and address. While the data is not entirely clear the attitude to gender seems to have changed over the period. Early almshouses might be designated for men, as at Frieston, or for women, as at Beamsley, or for equal numbers of each, as in the pre-seventeenth century foundations of the Bedehouse and Trinities at Pontefract [69, 73]. The combined provision of the Pontefract almshouses was impressive and would seem to have followed demographic trends in providing for men, more women, and some couples, with the proviso that a widowed spouse might then transfer to one of the other almshouses. Other instances of even-handed provision for men and women may be recognised architecturally as at Bentham [9] before its rebuild in 1900 and in the former premises at Drax [25] where men and women were neatly accommodated either side of the school whose scholars they were expected to board.

By the nineteenth century both census returns and popular parlance indicate that the majority of almshouse residents were women, often widows. Although only Thomas Palmer's foundation at Sedbergh was formally called the Widows' Hospital [86] others were sometimes spoken of in the same terms (although spinsters were not excluded). The Charity Commissioners, concerned with trustees' adherence to their charity's original objectives, found at Selby [87] that although theoretically open to men or women, as far as anyone could remember the residents were always women. This is open to more than one interpretation. Society's perceptions may have changed, reinforced by local custom, more women survived (despite the dangers of childbirth) into a physically but not economically independent old age, whilst – again emphasised by local practice –more women than men may have seen the almshouse as a goal. Booth's investigations into the elderly poor, quoted earlier, found a gender pattern: in Dewsbury, for instance, 'quite elderly women can earn a comfortable living by rag picking or at least tend children or do charing' (Booth, 1894, no. 68). Among the elderly workhouse inmates he found a preponderance of men, perhaps another indicator of the independence required of almshouse living.

Fig. 33 Excerpt from correspondence between Joseph Banks, MP, (trustee) and the agent on site at the Earl of Shrewsbury's Hospital, Sheffield. A double courtyard was proposed to allow seemly separation of men and women in the 1724 rebuilding scheme, on the previous site. *Sheffield Archives, Arundel Castle Manuscripts, S533/7.*

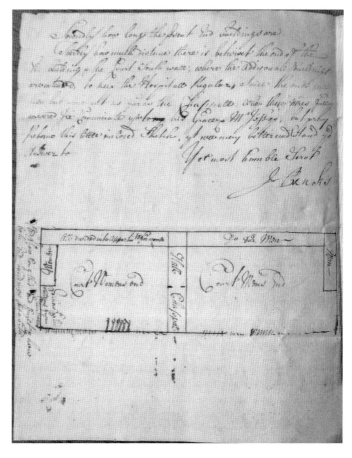

The almost universal requirement for a potential almsperson was local origins or at least local residence for a good length of time. The locality might be defined by the parish boundaries or named townships, or might be wider or narrower in accordance with the founder's inclinations. Subsequent population changes have made some of these restrictions unrealistic and it would seem that founders seldom considered the bigger picture, with the possible exception of the disparate parish of Ecclesfield where some such distinctions may have been made between the four almshouses [27–29, 90].

Overriding district boundaries might be landownership where the founder's family continued their patronage of the almshouse. Applicants to the Earl of Shrewsbury's Hospital in Sheffield [93] might stress their years of work and residence on the Earl's estates: William West had been an estate tenant for 38 years when he found himself 'totally unable to procure for himself the necessities of life' in 1867. His application was supported by 27 of his neighbours in Sheffield Park (ACM/S 533/9). Similarly a preference might be given to former employees or their widows, as at Wilshaw [114] or Saltaire [84]. Others were not excluded, but within a tight community the extent to which almspeople already knew one another must have affected the dynamics of the smaller almshouse community.

Former occupation could be another factor and again must have influenced the

Fig. 34 Potential almspeople. a) Charity Capper had been an outpensioner of the Earl of Shrewsbury's Hospital since first presenting her petition in 1851. From the 1860s this large foundation used forms to list applicants' occupation, place of origin, age, health and circumstances. b) The patron of Beamsley Hospital, Lord Thanet, presented new almswomen, Anne Cryor in 1686 and Martha Snell in 1728. (Bethemsley is an old form of Beamsley). *Sheffield Archives ACM, S533/9 (a); North Yorkshire County Record Office, PR/BNA 17/4/1 (b).*

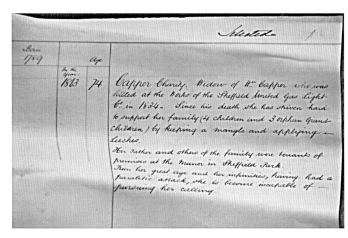

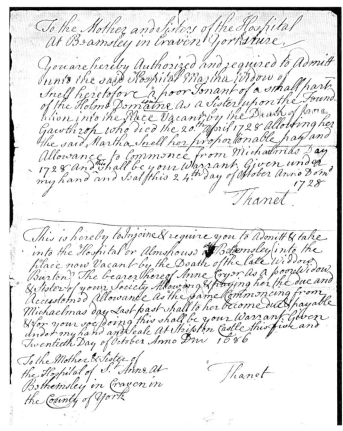

nature of the almshouse community both in terms of shared experience and previous position in the hierarchy. At the Victoria Almshouses in Wombwell [115], an early seventeenth-century foundation rebuilt and renamed in 1888, a preference was given to miners, although it is not known when this custom began, while Hollis's Hospital in Sheffield [91] came to favour applications from cutlers and their dependants. Also in Sheffield, in 1853 the local association of licensed victuallers established an 'asylum' [92] for their retired members. During the early twentieth century the trend towards occupationally-based almshouses increased nationally with large scale provision of Miners' Homes in County Durham and the Whiteley Village in Surrey. In Halifax the sweet manufacturers established the Mackintosh Homes while in 1868 George Rogers had retired from a successful lifetime in business in Bradford to enjoy the tranquillity and healthful atmosphere of Harrogate [39]. Here he provided for a dozen men and women, also tradespeople but with less to show for their endeavours.

Some criteria, it seems, remained unstated even if generally understood and applied. Almshouses were not there for the feckless, the dirty or the immoral. Instead they were fitting rewards for some of the respectable or 'deserving poor', many of whom were seen to have fallen on hard times through no fault of their own: ill-health or an accident causing loss of employment, the expense of bringing up a large family who were unable to reciprocate leading to exhaustion and penury. In some charities places were targeted at those belonging to a certain station in society.

These implicit criteria are evidenced from the mid-nineteenth century onwards through application letters, references and occasionally discussion among trustees recorded in their minute books. In some new Schemes (revised constitutions formalised by the Charity Commissioners) these criteria become explicit. Paucity of earlier evidence makes it impossible to be sure whether this had been the norm, or at least common practice, or whether it was a development of that period. Very few early foundation documents include this issue, although Thomas Ellis stated in 1557 that the six elderly almspeople at St. Thomas's Hospital in Doncaster [22] would be 'of good name and fame' and not 'common beggars' but those who had 'fallen into poverty by sickness or misfortune' (CC I, 107, 130). Ellis had already established a temporary lodging house for the town.

Countess Margaret attributed her foundation at Beamsley to her distress on observing the poor women in the streets of Skipton (DD 139) but this may have been a personal expression of care and responsibility rather than a reflection of a particular economic crisis. Her daughter is known to have found places for her former household servants in her own foundation at Appleby and some of these were literate (Spence, 1997). In 1902, the widow of the former clerk to the trustees at Sedbergh was herself considered an appropriate applicant (WDEC 18/2). The provisions of the 1834 Poor Law introduced a further factor, involving both status and finance, as poor relief might be construed as a form of income and its receipt as a social indicator. This will be discussed later in connection with pensions.

The expression most frequently encountered is that applicants should be 'of good conversation', for which 'decent and respectable' might be a modern translation.

Finally, some charities required religious observance as a criterion. This was most often Church of England, and although not universal appeared in foundation documents throughout the period. Only in one place, Sedbergh [86], was proof required in the form of the applicant's certificate of baptism. Not surprisingly, some otherwise deserving cases had lost this vital paper (WDEC 18/2). Elsewhere the intention is less clearcut, at least if it is to be understood in modern terms. Throughout the period church attendance was regarded as the norm. People met and were seen at church; it was an inseparable part of social life for the majority and a feature of the community. Values, hierarchical as much as moral, were reinforced: attendance might be seen as a sign of compliance with convention on a much wider front. In the particular context religion might be seen as the comforter of old age and an essential requisite for those approaching their end. Death was more frankly and frequently found as a part of life.

Despite the religious upheavals and diversity of the seventeenth century all known almshouse foundations from that period appear to conform to the established church. Were there puritan or other dissenter foundations, not overt for legal reasons? Thomas Hollis [91] was a dissenter, although the 1726 trust deed prepared by his son made no denominational restrictions, however applied in practice. The scene changed and in the nineteenth century non-conformity and philanthropy (as shown by the Crossley family and others) was a distinctive and distinguished combination. Half a dozen West Riding almshouses in the industrial areas of Sheffield, Halifax and Bradford were certainly non-conformist in origin, although their admission criteria were not exclusive. In Wakefield the forthright Dr. Caleb Crowther [108] ensured that non-conformists would have a place in his almshouse after hearing of the exclusion of 'an honest and industrious old man' (JG, letter), a Methodist, from another establishment.

The importance – or otherwise – of religious attendance might continue for the almshouse resident, especially in those few houses with their own chapel on site. This will be discussed later as part of almshouse life. Meanwhile it may be sufficient to say that the impression gained from the documents is of religious attendance as some form of accountability by the residents to any charity that required it and a visual proof of the founder's beneficence when the almspeople attended the local church en masse. It does not render almshouses, any more than other charitable creations such as schools, bridges and markets, as religious institutions. A very few founders were churchmen, but when almshouses did develop parochial links these emerged as part of their subsequent administration.

The fortunate individual who complied with the charity's criteria might yet have to await a vacancy. The length of the waiting list reflected the relative merits of the particular almshouse's facilities in comparison with any other provision within the area at the time (pers. com.) and could fluctuate accordingly. Some beneficiaries continued to enjoy their places for a couple of decades or even longer. Actual age and longevity for almspeople is hard to track as registers, where retained, do not offer many continuous sequences and the census returns from 1851 onwards are not consistent in their format and, of course, residents could come and go within the decade unrecorded. What is apparent is that a fair number of almspeople were already well into their seventies or early eighties on moving in. During the 1850s those entering the Shrewsbury Hospital [93] ranged in age between 65 and 89 for men and 67 and 92 for women, although this includes a number who were already outpensioners and effectively on the 'housing list' (ACM/S 533/9). The inscribed panels in the porches of the Salt Hospital [84] show residents between 1868 and 1878 achieving an average of five years in the almshouse, with an increasing number living into their eighties. (True figures for longevity and period of residence should be higher, as the panels record deaths and not those still present at the end of the decade).

Did the comfort and security of decent and healthy living conditions with permanent tenure encourage longevity or was it rather those who had already proved to be survivors who benefited: cause and effect are inseparable. More data analysis could establish

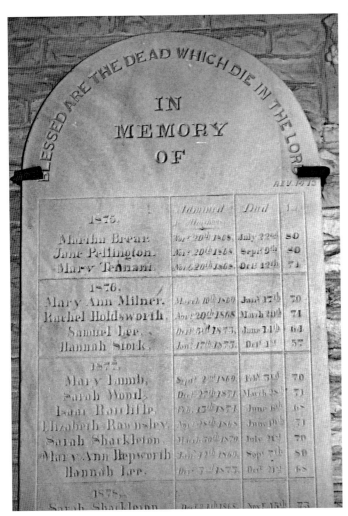

whether almshouse residents did live longer than their peers in the community. Although the almsperson would be looking after him or herself initially health could decline and then the role of the almshouse becomes less clear. Who should take responsibility for a sick or incapacitated resident or one who is described briefly in the minute books as 'behaving unsuitably', failing to keep their house clean and hygienic, or occasionally 'insane', possibly suffering from Alzheimer's disease?

The almshouse community itself might give support and this was recommended by some founders, Mary Bellamy at Rotherham [83] advising that 'the others shall be aiding and assisting' any sick almswoman (CC, i, 401). Friends or relatives could call and run errands; the accessible location of the almshouse was important.

In only a few almshouses were there any resident staff (see Table 5) and they were not employed as nurses, although they could call for medical assistance. Certainly almshouses were not sheltered housing by the strict definition of assistance on call 24 hours. And so a live-in carer, perhaps niece or grand-daughter, might join the almsperson. This presented a quandary for the trustees, responsible for ensuring that no extraneous persons – lodgers, impecunious or opportunistic relatives or hangers-on – received benefits to which they were not entitled. Minutes record such individuals who were instructed to leave, although the census returns demonstrate their presence. In other cases a request was properly made to the trustees and the carer granted the right of residence (but no other benefits) so long as their almsperson remained. At Hemsworth [41] Mary Bailey who had previously cared for 'the blind Brother' later became an almswoman herself (C 345/1/3).

Table 5 Facilities and support (so far as known)

Pension, cash	Other benefits (fuel, etc.)	Communal room (chapel, dining room etc.)	Staff (warden or senior almsperson)
85	35+	24	22

Who took responsibility?

By now it will be clear that an almshouse was not a simple self-regulatory organism; that duties and administrative obligations were present, and that it was people outside the almshouse who were generally responsible for making decisions and implementing them. Much of this fell to members of the inevitable committees (the trustees) who took over after the founder's death, but first something should be said of the founders themselves who were legally in the happy position of making whatever idiosyncratic plans they chose, so long as funding was included. Perhaps the 'typical' founder could be described as at least moderately wealthy, with no direct heirs (or sufficient to spare) who cared about the wellbeing of the local community and wished to benefit it in a visible and enduring manner, often through the provisions of his or her will. That might describe many other charitable donors, and indeed the individuals who founded or supported almshouses often did contribute to other worthwhile causes within the same local dimension. A few founders established almshouses during their lifetimes: the Gascoigne sisters [1], for example, were still in their thirties and single; Joseph Crossley [37] in middle age was closely involved in his project. As shown in Chapter Three, several almshouses were created in memory of another family member and some of those ideas may have been discussed and plans made before the event.

In terms of social status almshouse founders were a mixed bunch, although unlikely to overlap with their beneficiaries. Aristocrats, gentry, burgesses and businessmen predominate, with a sprinkling of professionals and a good number of women, either widows or wealthy in their own right. In a few instances the founding family maintained a link with their charity through the generations; some such as the Parkers at Waddington [103] still do so. 'Local boy made good' would describe some who were new or aspiring gentry and had left home for the city but remembered their roots in old age, and perhaps were happy to remind the stay-at-homes of their success. Joseph Smith [100] returned to Thornton-in-Craven after a banking career in London; Richard Read [25], an orphan who went to sea and became a shipowner, benefited his native Drax. Ferrand Spence was a London businessman who formed a Craven connection. The story – which may be apocryphal – is that he was lost on the moors, received hospitality from an elderly woman, and set up the almshouses at Carleton-in-Craven in gratitude. He may have come from the Midlands, as the terms of the charity included beneficiaries from Market Bosworth, although few cared to move so far north [15].

Archbishop Holgate's connection with Hemsworth [41] is unknown, although birthplace seems likely. Created Archbishop of York by Edward Tudor, his position as a married clergyman became untenable under Mary. Perhaps the uncertainty of the times and the need to find a worthy resting place for his considerable wealth outside of the royal coffers led to this charitable activity. Individual motivation and combinations of philanthropy and self-interest must be personal to each founder. Beyond unavoidable observation of the vulnerable and needy, an ageing founder might well contemplate the perils and concerns of old age and dwell on visions of permanence and eternity, creating a living human memorial 'in perpetuum' as Bryan Cooke wrote at Arksey [5] in 1660. A small number of foundations or refoundations were a group response to an event or occasion: Holmfirth, Crigglestone and Horbury were mentioned in the previous chapter.

When founders named executors or trustees in their wills it was these people, and in turn their descendants (either hereditary or in terms of their position) who made any decisions not already documented or conveyed to them personally. They had the essential duty of putting the funds to the best use in pursuit of the charity's interests.

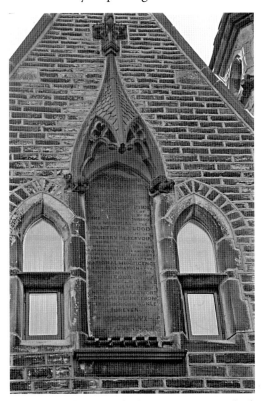 

Fig. 36 The disaster and subsequent generosity leading to the foundation of the almshouse at Holmfirth: a) flood and funding are recorded on the façade; b) contributing districts and their trustee representatives are listed above the gateway. *Photos: author.*

Briefly, this could involve purchase of land, both as a building site and to produce rents as endowment, investment (and after successive bank crashes during the nineteenth century government stock known as consols were favoured) building and rebuilding, ongoing repairs and maintenance, payment of any rates and later insurance and utilities' bills, and payment of pensions in cash or kind to the almspeople and payments to any 'staff', such as a clergyman for preaching special sermons, a clerk or lawyer (if they had one) and themselves for holding an annual dinner, although only some charities had these requirements.

Some detail differs but present-day charity trustees will find most of this familiar, allowing for more legislation but also more professional advice. Trustees collectively must have sufficient time, interest, local knowledge, goodwill and business sense. Individually they might come from a similar background to their founder, but where composition was specified by occupation they could include those pillars of the community, the vicar – another guarantee of permanence – and possibly the schoolmaster. By the later nineteenth century local authority representatives had a place. In small communities, however, roles and responsibilities often overlapped and devolved on the same few willing and able to undertake them. Despite the number of women founders, trustees did not include women members before the early twentieth century when Miss Kitson battled through two decades to replace ranges with modern stoves in Mary Potter's Hospital [59] (WYAS,L, uncatalogued).

Economic fluctuation affects charities as it does businesses, positively or adversely. Growth of income may be sufficient for expansion so that more units are built to increase the number of beneficiaries, lesser growth permits improved facilities or the residents might benefit more directly through a pension increase. Trustees make these choices. Not surprisingly, over the period some have been more competent and more active than others. A number of high profile scandals where charitable funds were diverted from the poor to the wealthy in a breach of trust acquired national infamy. The events at St. Cross in Hampshire inspired Anthony Trollope's novel, *The Warden*. In the West Riding problems were uncovered at Hemsworth in the 1630s and 1690s (C 3435/1/26, C 345/3/1) and documentary evidence from some other charities suggests more localised but strongly felt issues where charity was abused in being treated as private patronage by the trustees (PR/PRL 18/9/4).

The Charity Commissioners' investigations of the 1830s were in part a response to these problems and the public feeling that they generated. A programme of regulation was begun, formalised through new Schemes from which any deviation required official assent, committing to paper accrued custom as well as original aims, but with greater clarity and consistency, and sometimes gaining a contemporary gloss in deciding on the relevance of some founders' stated intentions. Such intervention might be seen as interference and a protracted battle was waged in Doncaster over the Corporation's arrangements for Stock's Almshouses [23] (Jackson, 1881) and nearly a century later at Long Preston [63] (PR/PRL 18/8/18). Trustees' correspondence and the local press give a vivid picture of local issues, human failings and 'negotiation'.

Apart from these occasional dramas, the most common problem was lack of cash. Some investments were unwise, over-cautious or just unlucky; some lands were blessed by coal mines and railways, valuable commodities. The crucial factor was the extent of endowment. The charities that collapsed – often literally so in terms of their property – were the unendowed or under-endowed almshouses without funds to cover maintenance or provide residents' pensions. Some of these charities were mere undocumented ruins and memories by the time of the Charity Commissioners' visits in the 1890s. But in other places a sense of community and awareness of local needs led the local authority to take over. In addition to those already mentioned, Greenwood's Hospital at Ardsley [5] a sixteenth-century foundation, was maintained by the parish until 1837, and the Bead House at Featherstone [30] and Clarkson's Charity at Ferrybridge [31] were small almshouses similarly supported. In such circumstances what had been personal charities came to be seen as community resources, merging with less specific poors' houses (free or low-rent parish housing for the needy on a temporary basis) while the poor rate was relied upon in place of pensions, causing a further blurring of status.

Were almspeople regulated?

To return to the trustees' responsibilities, after initial selection of the almspeople and an ongoing care (to varying degrees) for their wellbeing, compliance with the terms of the charity and its good reputation were important matters; these were the residents' duties too. The number of rules and the extent to which they impinged on daily life varied considerably. For the most part, founders may have hoped that rigorous selection plus gratitude (and an awareness of the alternative if the ultimate sanction of eviction was applied) would ensure a satisfactory community. Indeed this must have been so as it is the rarity with which problems enter the minute books that makes them conspicuous, when 'it was agreed that one of the trustees should speak to Mrs. X', a formula of reluctance to interfere. A few founders attempted to regulate their charges' lives, with rules kept always in view and a list of fines scaled to possible misdemeanours. Elizabeth Rand [12] who built in Bradford in 1876, formulated a lengthy set of rules stipulating a self-regulatory curfew of 10pm, an embargo on carrying on any trade or hanging out washing in view of passers-by. She retained the right to inspect individual residents' homes to ensure that they were well kept, with chimneys swept regularly and 'approved' furniture (B 363.5). Although the tone suggests that Elizabeth was a control freak, how intrusive were the rules?

A curfew was specified at several almshouses, with seasonal hours – 8pm to 7am in winter and 9pm to 6am in summer at Waddington – reflecting safety of movement before the installation of streetlighting. Alternatively it could be perceived as institutional interference into personal liberty and an irritation in that it could only be policed by gossip. Only in places with a warden on the premises or an outer door that could be locked was a curfew enforceable; no mention of infringement appears in the minute books. The issue of no trade would seem integral to the purpose of the almshouse, but in conjunction with the mention of visible laundry may refer to that staple of unskilled female employment, taking in washing, as well as to the proprieties. Victorian concern added the thought of titillating underwear to earlier almshouse rules designed to prevent cohabitation or over-familiarity between almsmen and women.

Certain almshouses required church attendance and a pew could be set aside for the almspeople in the parish church (pers. com.) unless prayers were read in their own chapel or other communal area within the building. This might take place two

Fig. 37 Duty and responsibilities: a) a bond stating the obligations incurred by Sarah Wood from Midgley on entering Nathaniel Waterhouse's almshouse in 1699; b) a detail from the 1888 Rules of the Gascoigne Almshouse where this symbol of Christian charity accompanied exceptional restrictions on movement, visiting hours and allocation of 'pocket money'. *WYAS,C HAS 672/46 (a); copy WYAS,L. WYL 1002 Acc. 2379 (b).*

or three times a week, with a local clergyman officiating, or in the case of a combined almshouse and school, the schoolmaster would have this duty. Failure to attend, unless genuinely ill, was a visible form of backsliding, and fines were stipulated. The 1665 rules at Beamsley Hospital [8] state: 'that prayers be daily said' and that mother and sisters must 'give their constant attendance and none of them to be absent at any time unless in case of sickness or other urgent occasions' with the unattractive and surely unnecessary Clause 10 that for 'wilfully breaking any of the rules' a fortnight's worth of the offender's pension should be redistributed amongst the more virtuous residents, with a payment 'to the informer' (DD 139).

These were active requirements of the residents, but the majority of rules and exhortations were intended to achieve a quiet life for all concerned. Almsmen at Tancred's Hospital in Whixley [113] founded in 1763 were expected to 'behave with decency and good manners' and must not be 'troublesome in the society' as a communal lifestyle was envisaged here (DD 160). At Frieston Hospital [49] it was expected that the brothers should 'godly, charitably, lovingly, gently, quietly, brotherly behave' amongst themselves and 'to all men humbly and gently' (DD 154).

It was exceptional for relationships to deteriorate to the extent that they did in Long Preston [63] during the 1840s. This was not due to any contravention of the rules regarding church attendance or wearing uniform (to be discussed later) but reads more like a personality clash that led to a stand-off. The minutes note that Jane Taylor was to be expelled for 'wilfully and disobediently harbouring a young woman in her house after divers admonitions' to which she had responded in a 'disrespectful and insubordinate manner'. Another trustee undertook negotiations and Jane stayed. The trustees brought in a new set of more stringent rules, backed up by fines, presumably as a deterrent, but these were subsequently declared invalid (PR/PRL 18/9/5).

Residence was an important rule for almshouse charities to avoid abuse of the charity and dereliction of its property (as mentioned in the previous chapter). It also implies a care for any absent residents, through a knowledge of their whereabouts. Over the period it became common practice for almspeople to apply to the trustees with details of any intended time away, which was not expected to exceed one or two weeks.

These, then, were the constraints on almshouse life, designed to maintain a contented and respectable community. The extent of implementation is hard to assess and rules may not have seemed unduly onerous. Some trustees would have been more directly involved than others, visiting the almspeople from a proper and kindly sense of care, not looking for problems. It is clear that there was great reluctance to apply sanctions, with the ultimate one of removal occasionally recommended not as punishment but on medical grounds.

Did almspeople have the opportunity to make rules for their own community or to make representations to those who did? The records do little to help here, and until the latter part of the period registers or receipts show many almspeople signing their name with a cross. However in the case of some older incorporated charities the consent of the residents was required for any major changes, especially involving finance. This applied at Beamsley, where the mother had charge of the seal although there is no evidence of consultation. Important issues might lead to representations being made by the residents collectively. This is known to have occurred at Joseph Crossley's Almshouses

[37] shortly after their construction when a request was made for lighting on the dark passages and paths to the rear of the buildings, the access to the privies. This was apparently turned down and individual lanterns offered instead (pers. com.). Joseph took a close personal interest in his foundation and in other respects did encourage residents' participation. A chapel was provided on-site where meetings were to be led by ministers or lay readers from the non-conformist denominations, chosen jointly by the almspeople (see Fig. 40). This in turn must have generated meetings and discussion, suggesting a communal structure akin to a residents' association. The meeting room attached to the chapel still houses social events. It remains open to question whether almspeople were, in practice, any more regulated than their contemporaries as tenants and employees, often dependent on the good opinion of their social superiors and expected to show suitable deference.

What were the benefits?

However, it is possible to be more positive about the benefits that almspeople received. Already mentioned is the essential of a secure, maintained and rent free home, generally in pleasant surroundings. The distinction that has been made here between almshouses (buildings) and almshouse charities is intended to emphasise the package provided by the charities. Long before Lloyd George's contribution to the welfare state in 1908, almspeople received pensions. Pensions, again, spelt security, a feeling of self-respect and a moderate degree of independence. They allowed a modest standard of living in food, clothing and other personal necessities.

Nevertheless pensions did vary considerably in amount and purchasing power. Where foundation deeds named the sum and date of distribution, no allowance was made for future inflation or changing habits. The figure was usually an annual one and distribution quarterly. If there was a senior figure on the premises, he or she counted out the cash – in the case of the mother at Beamsley, handing it out directly from the chest in her room where the rents were paid in. Countess Margaret was fully aware of the importance of a regular income and sensible budget: she herself had struggled with debts due to her husband's improvidence and stipulated that pensions were to be paid 'constantly' so that 'none of the sisters do run on the score in the town' (Spence, 1997). But there are no shopping lists or orders for group purchasing to indicate the adequacy of the pension or what was bought.

The following examples of initial pensions (annual figures) indicate the differences between charities: 10s. at St. Thomas's (1557), £5. at Arksey (1660), £4. at Waddington (1701), £18. at James's (1723), £10. at Freeman's (1836). Later adjustments were up to the trustees, depending on funds available and their awareness of the costs of living for the almspeople. Certainly examples can be found of gradual increases, and further work could relate this to contemporary living costs. Trustees might have another reason to increase pensions, on the lines of dividends to shareholders, if the charity had surplus wealth. This led to the vexed question as to the amount that was suitable for the social level of an almsperson. After protracted deliberation driven by local opinion freely aired in the press, pensions at Hemsworth [41] were increased under the Scheme of 1857 to £40, to take full effect from 1870 (CC, v, 224). Hunter had noted opinions here as early as the 1820s when concern was expressed that almspeople would be unable to cope with their new-found wealth, either spending lavishly or hoarding sums to pass on to others (Hunter, 1828–30). This charity also supported a master – a resident cleric and manager – who needed £550 to accomplish his duties and maintain a suitable lifestyle in the free six-bedroom house with stables.

But an argument that became increasingly tendentious in the later nineteenth century was over the relationship between pensions and poor relief. The question was asked whether anyone was entitled to both charitable assistance and benefits paid from the poor rate (effectively, by the taxpayer) and furthermore whether the sort of person who had been in receipt of relief (unless in exceptional and temporary circumstances) was eligible for an almshouse place. Some of the social nuances are apparent in the Charity Commissioners' comments, for instance at Rawmarsh [79] where rebuilding in 1894 was accompanied by a new Scheme and the recommendation that 'no doubt the overseers [of the poor] will review these cases now that the stipends have been so largely increased' (CC, i, 51). Meanwhile they were satisfied with Marsland's Almshouses in Wakefield [106] where the 'main benefit' was 'to be found in the provision of clean and comfortable accommodation for poor women who have small means of their own' (CC, v, 679). (See Fig. 91 for further details). The 'small means' of residents at the cash-strapped Bead House in Featherstone [30] came from childminding and shoe repairs. The pension therefore had a defining effect on eligible or feasible residents of an almshouse. But local decisions were apparently made in the light of local circumstances. Certainly some trustees were content for their almspeople to be supported partially by the poor rate and at least charity could be seen to reduce the overall burden.

The pensions discussed so far are cash sums, but about a quarter of the charities investigated (and possibly more) also made payments in kind (see Table 5). Warmth and cooked meals were essential for the elderly residents' health and fuel was a major outlay. Many almshouse charities record the delivery of 'a cart of coal at Christmas'. The record is seldom more detailed so that it is impossible to be sure of quantities and division between residents. The ubiquitous chimneys should be a reminder of the demand for solid fuel to cook and heat water all year round. As gas and then electricity

Fig. 38 Archbishop Holgate's Hospital. The master's house, also in banded brickwork but on a different scale, is entered through the triple arched loggia. The house is close to the upper almshouse range but forms a separate structure with its own driveway. *Photo: author.*

replaced wood and coal, payments in kind were commuted to an addition to the pension: at Barber's Almshouses in Gawber [33] the 5s 9d. weekly pension rose to 7s. in 1892 in lieu of coal (BB 22/8).

The other large if less frequent expenditure was on clothing and a smaller number of charities (excluding later foundations) gave this kind of assistance. The frequency of replacement varied and where accounts show costs of material and dressmaking charges men's clothes tended to cost more. Some founders liked to add their distinctively dressed almspeople to their image of the well-ordered house. Sir John Lewis at Ledsham [53] clothed his almsmen in blue frock coat and waistcoat, flannel shirt, silk hat, stockings and boots. More often the founder merely specified 'a coat or gown' of a certain colour (white at Hemsworth, grey at Drax, blue lined with green at Linton) and as a traditional style became customary and noticeably old-fashioned, clothing became identified as uniform. Buttons or a sleeve badge presented the almsperson in the founder's livery. Changing attitudes in the twentieth century saw such clothing first relegated to special occasions and then abandoned.

Harder to pin down and quantify are the provision of food for the almspeople (indicated in the records for Frieston and Waddington up till the eighteenth century); donations forthcoming from other local charities for the poor, especially for clothing and blankets; seasonal events and social gatherings in the community; and individual gifts. A near neighbour of the almshouses at Pledwick [68] recalled her mother 'baking

Fig. 39 Clothing and furniture: a) a drawing of the sleeve badge worn on the gown at Hemsworth, made when additional badges were required after the extensions of 1914; b) one of the chairs originally provided for each resident, now in the communal room at Joseph Crossley's Almshouses. *Trustee Collection (a); photo: author (b).*

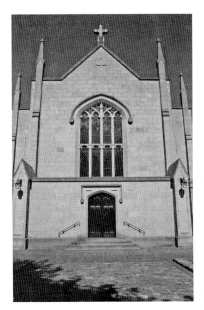

Fig. 40 Some foundations included a chapel on site. a) The chapel at the centre of the Shrewsbury Hospital complex. b) The home of the governor/chaplain adjoining some of the Shrewsbury almshouses. c) The first floor chapel and meeting room above one room units at Joseph Crossley's Almshouses. *Photos: author.*

for the old ladies' (pers. com.). From the later nineteenth century minute books show several charities taking out subscriptions for nursing care and retaining medical officers. As stated earlier, health care was not seen as an integral or necessarily appropriate part of the almshouse package; changing social expectations made these new arrangements both possible and realistic, at least for some larger charities. At Waddington after the

1895 rebuilding [103] a nurse was installed on a small monthly salary with the resources of a dispensary, although this was a short-lived venture (TC).

Staff have been mentioned as occasionally present at almshouses and their roles need to be clarified. Residential staff, known in modern terminology as wardens, are found here called variously mother, matron, master (with a managerial responsibility), secretary (to the charity), schoolmaster (in combined charities) or porter (responsible primarily for premises). As the person on the spot they must have been seen to have a catch-all caring role; dividing lines between what was undertaken personally and what was referred to the trustees are not clear or consistent. Taking into account changes over time, about twenty almshouses included some such person but status and duties clearly differed between someone who was essentially an almsperson with additional duties, recognised in his or her pension, and a professional man employed by the trustees to cope with day-to-day running of the almshouse, accommodated and salaried, but not automatically in a permanent position.

Another individual on the books of some almshouse charities, but not residential, was a clergyman – in practice often the local vicar or curate – frequently termed reader. Foundation documents that stipulated residents' attendance at prayers on the premises set aside an allowance for the reader and sometimes stipulated days and times. Daily prayers at 8 or 9am were specified at Beamsley in 1665, were still read three times weekly by a schoolmaster from Skipton in the late nineteenth century and were recorded, with note of hymns and travelling expenses on a twice weekly pattern up till 1954 (PR/BNA 17/4). Mary Brown who founded the almshouses at Grindleton [34] in 1860 stipulated that the vicar should call twice a week to read prayers. While the reader often received a fairly generous payment for his services – equal to the almsperson's annual pension – he might find himself by default becoming more closely involved as a channel of communication between residents and trustees. The inclusion of the local clergyman on many almshouse committees has already been noted.

Finally, and by way of summary, it should be said that despite intriguing individual differences between almshouse charities and the people involved, what was provided was a means of secure and independent living for such poor and elderly people as satisfied the criteria and obtained a place. The Directory following Chapter Five gives more details.

Chapter 5

Conclusion

Before moving on, it may be useful to summarise the foregoing chapters. While the Directory lists the almshouse charities known in the West Riding between 1600 and 1900, for some there is little more than a name, for others extensive documentation and for about half the historic buildings themselves survive. It is hoped that these supporting chapters aid the reader, whether in pursuit of a particular almshouse, locality, period or style of building, as each of these may gain another dimension from this investigation behind the scenes.

It has been found that two main strands of building layout co-existed – the row and the courtyard – as well as less common centripetal and semi-detached forms. Almost all the buildings fall within the identified 'almshouse genre', a development of the 'dignified vernacular' in which local and homely cottage features partake of certain polite or civic elements, both in detailing and their more substantial nature.

The statements made by the physical presence are echoed in the charities' foundation deeds and regulations. Residents should be respectable, orderly and deserving, appreciative of their good fortune and conformist as regards society's expectations of them. The most vital invisible factor is the pension, and both it and continued property maintenance depend on endowments and the good service of trustees. Taken individually, almshouses are slight ameliorations to the widespread poverty of old age. They function on a human scale rather than an institutional one and their arbitrary distribution and parochial scope limit their possible contribution.

Fig. 41 Victoria Memorial (Worrill's) Almshouses at Crigglestone. Rebuilt in 1901, this is one of the smallest rows. One of the three residents is setting out for a day with her friend. *Photo: author.*

Yet their influence is disproportionate to the number of beneficiaries. For several hundred years they have provided models of accommodation and services tailored to identified needs, offering independent living and the peace of mind arising from security and a sense of permanence. Notwithstanding the benefits of independence, they have retained characteristics of the self-contained community even whilst early elements of communal living have diminished.

Almshouse charities represent a package of essential support. The views of earlier almspeople were not recorded; present residents comment appreciatively on the special character of their homes and the good condition of house and garden. The almshouse building is a continuing monument to founder and residents and a reminder to both local and wider community of the values they embody. The reader is now equipped with a broader perspective and historical context in which to place individual examples. These are numerous and varied and may be found throughout the West Riding of Yorkshire.

The West Riding of Yorkshire

50 miles

Sedbergh

Ripon

Bentham

Knaresborough

Harrogate

Skipton   York

Ilkley

Waddington   Thornton-in-Craven   Leathley   Linton

Otley

Tadcaster

Cawood

Saltaire   Aberford

Leeds

Bradford   Ledsham

Halifax   Methley   Drax

Sowerby   Wakefield   Pontefract   Snaith

Horbury   Kirkthorpe

Huddersfield

Almondbury   Flockton Crigglestone   Hemsworth

Holmfirth   Arksey

Barnsley   Doncaster

Wentworth

Ecclesfield   Rotherham

Tickhill

Sheffield

Appendix 1

The Directory

Almshouses are listed alphabetically by place. Grid references are given where possible.
- **indicates a pre-1901 building still present.**

References: CC refers to the Charity Commissioners' *Endowed Charities* reports of 1897–99.

1. ABERFORD •
Gascoigne Almshouses

Fig. 42 Gascoigne almshouses, Aberford, 2004. *Photo: author.*

On the village outskirts, on the former Great North Road, grid ref. SE 433 364.
Founded 1844 by the Misses Gascoigne, sisters in their thirties.

Two storey enhanced row of 8 units, each one up, one down, with internal staircase. Chapel at one end, dining hall at the other, all accessed off a corridor, reached from the entrance hall. Service area and staff accommodation to rear of dining hall. Rampant Gothic, including clock tower with battlements, pinnacles, vacant niche. Stained glass in entrance hall depicts charity. Large gardens front and rear; gate lodge.
Architect: George Fowler Jones of York. Cost of building: £40,000.
Residents: 4 M + 4 F, local. Matron, maid. Visiting chaplain. Pension, other support.
Rules include cleaning, gardening, and dining together.
Now business premises.
Refs: CC, iv, pp. 4–10; Maclure, A. c.1845. *View of the Monumental Almshouses at Aberford* (lithograph, Lotherton Hall); WYAS,L. WYL 1002/acc.2379; Pevsner, 1967, p.69; White, 2004, pp. 3–4.

2. ACKWORTH •
Mary Lowther's Hospital
In the village centre, facing the green and the stocks, grid ref. SE 441 179.
Founded 1741.
Single storey stone row of 6 units, one room

Fig. 43 Mary Lowther's Hospital, Ackworth, seen across the village green with the water pump in the foreground. The rear projection of the roofline indicates the master's house. *Photo: author.*

and pantry each, with central block forming the schoolhouse with master's accommodation to rear. Unadorned but with Classical symmetry, central pediment, Gibbs door. Close to the road, with garden behind.

Plaque: 'Mary Lowther erected and endowed this hospital for a schoolmaster and 6 poor women 1741'.

Residents: 6 F, over 40, local. Pension; Mrs. Surtees' benefaction from 1801.

Now private houses.

Refs: CC, v, pp. 2, 11–12; Pevsner, 1967, p. 69; Pontefract and Castleford Express, 1982.

3. ALMONDBURY, near Huddersfield •

Robert Nettleton's Almshouses

Old School Lane, grid ref. SE 151 169.

Founded 1613, building recorded 1727 at Broken Cross, near the workhouse.

Rebuilt on present site 1863.

Single storey row of 6 units, each one room and bed alcove. Stone, long and short work to doors and three-light mullioned windows, Welsh slate roof. Narrow strip garden.

Plaque: built 'by the trustees of Robert Nettleton esquire in the year 1863 for the perpetual relief of the poor of Almondbury. The money was granted out of the charity's funds at the annual meeting of the trustees on the 27th day of September 1860. Joseph Armitage, Chairman. The land was given by Sir John William Ramsden, baronet.'

Residents: 6 M/F, local. Pension.

Refs: CC, iii, pp. 715–23; WYAS,K. KC643, 644; Sykes, 1992, pp. 71-75.

4. ARDSLEY, near Wakefield

Greenwood's Hospital

Probably opposite Greenwood's house, near the waterworks at Westerton.

Founded 1593. Repaired by the parish until 1837, empty in 1892.

Residents: 3 F.

Refs: CC, v, pp. 741–2.

5. ARKSEY, near Doncaster •

Bryan Cooke's Almshouses

Beside the school in the old village centre, grid ref. SE 580 069.

Founded 1660.

Single storey stone courtyard, three-light mullioned windows, steeply pitched tiled roof. 12 units on 3 sides with central through passage, high wall and pedimented gateway. Unadorned and symmetrical. Small garden and allotments to rear.

Inscription over gateway (badly worn) records that a sum of money was invested in 1660 for '12 paupertate et senio maximi laborantium' (sic) in the parish of Arksey, to receive a pension of £5 per annum 'in perpetuum'. Lower plaque records rebuilding of gateway by great-nephew.

Residents: 12 M/F, local. Pension, augmented by Brewer 1687.

Refs. CC, i, pp. 8 9, 15–17; Jordan, 1961, p. 280; Pevsner, 1967, p. 83.

6. BARKISLAND

The Almshouse

Small foundation for the aged poor, unknown date, demolished mid-nineteenth century.

Refs. CC, iii, p. 248.

7. BAWTRY

Forster's Charity

Foundation for 2 F, unknown date. Orchard, but no pension.

Refs. CC, i, pp. 40–1.

8. BEAMSLEY •

Beamsley Hospital

7 miles from Skipton on the Harrogate road, grid ref. SE 082 531.

Founded 1593 by Margaret, Countess of Cumberland, completed 1620s–1630s by her daughter, Lady Anne Clifford.

Earlier building stone and stone slates, centripetal, 6 + 1 units accessed from central chapel. Single storey, but chapel lit from raised lantern roof. Later building same materials, almost symmetrical stone row of 6 units, some with second room in roof space. Unadorned. Central archway leads to garden, path to early building, and demolished laundry. Set back behind wall and narrow garden.

Plaque: 'This almshouse was founded by that excellent Countess Margaret wife of George Clifford in 1593, and was more perfectly finished by her only child, Anne, Countess of Pembroke. God's name be praised'. Coats of arms.

Residents: 12 F and mother, local. Visiting reader. Pension, some other support.

Now owned by Landmark Trust as holiday accommodation and private housing.

Refs: CC, ii, pp. 727, 763; NY. PR/BNA 17/4; WYAS,Y. DD139; Dawson, 1882; Pacey, Bayer, 2001; Percy, 1990; Pevsner, 1967, p. 99; Spence, 1997.

9. BENTHAM, north of Bowland •

Collingwood's Almshouses

On the main street in High Bentham, grid ref. SD 675 694.

Founded 1726 by William Collingwood on his death, aged 31.

Originally two rows facing, M and F, with separate wash house. Rebuilt 1900, one very long low rendered row, sash windows and slate roof,

Fig. 44 Collingwood's Almshouses, Bentham. The gable end of the long row faces the street accoutred with a plaque for the 1900 rebuild, the street name and strategically placed seating. The glazed porches are recent additions. *Photo: author.*

definitely unadorned. End-on to the street with small garden beyond.

Plaque records rebuilding with additional funds from Mrs. Titterington.

Residents: 6 M + 6 F, local, C. of E. Pension.

Refs: CC, ii, pp. 20, 26, 37; NY. PR/BNL 11/5; Bibby, 1910.

10. **BINGLEY**
Rhodes Charity
Off Priesthorpe Lane in the old settlement, above the modern town.

Founded 1784 by Sarah Rhodes, possibly in succession to a trust by Thomas Dobson.

Residents: 5 'ancient poor persons', local.

Refs. CC, ii, pp. 56, 84; Dodd, 1958.

11. **BRADFORD** •
Melbourne Almshouses
On Sawrey Place, off Little Horton Lane, near the Friends Meeting House, grid ref. SE 157 316.

Founded 1845 by Mary Rathmell, née Melbourne.

Single storey stone row with low pitched roof of shaped slates. Gables symmetrically placed front and ends, central projection with through archway, finial and crest above. Stonework rough, unadorned. Small garden.

Residents: 8 F, usually Quaker. Probably a pension, fuel.

Rules: be kind and obliging to neighbours, curfew, worship.

Refs. Hustwick, 1957–58, no. 84.

12. **BRADFORD** •
Rand's Almshouses
On McTurk Grove, off Whetley Street, Manningham, grid ref. SE 155 338.

Founded 1876 by Elizabeth Rand.

Single storey stone row enhanced by two storey wings with gablets to the side faces, accommodating single and two storey units. Gothic with stepped gable over central pair of doors, entwined initials JER, chamfered corners to wings, blank escutcheons. No garden remaining.

Plaque: '1876 These almshouses were built by Elizabeth Rand in loving accordance with the

Fig. 45 Melbourne Almshouses, Bradford. a) View of three of the units in the row, with gablet and central archway. The roof has retained its decorative shaped tiles although modern porches sit within the hood moulds for the doors. b) Stonework has suffered badly from weathering and pollution: the crest is accompanied by a replacement foundation plaque. *Photos: author.*

73

Fig. 46 Rand's Almshouses, Bradford. a) The symmetrical row has two storeys at either end to accommodate two units each. Re-use as private housing accounts for the skylights and satellite dish. b) Detail of the Gothic doorway for the two central units, with the founder's initials beneath the foundation plaque (now removed). *Photos: author.*

wishes of her husband John Rand who died June 27 AD 1873'.

Residents: 8 M/F/C, employee first choice, deposit. Pension,

Rules lengthy including curfew, no trade, no washing to be hung out.

Now privately occupied.

Refs. BL. B363.5; Hustwick, 1957–58, no. 67. (Some confusion in CC entry for [15])

13. BRADFORD ●
Ripley Almshouses
On New Cross Street, between the railway, Bowling Park and the former dye works, grid ref. SE 168 312.

Founded 1857 by Edward and Hannah Ripley and rebuilt 1881 by their son.

Two storey stone row, slate roof. No central feature but a protruding gable each end, tall chimneys. Doors paired with ivy leaf decoration in the spandrel, otherwise unadorned. Strip garden and to rear.

Inscriptions: LHS 'Bowling Dye Works almshouses AD MDCCCLVII', RHS 'Rebuilt in memory of Edward and Hannah Ripley AD MDCCCLXXXI'.

Residents: 10 M/F, employee first choice. Pension. Now privately owned.

Refs. WYAS,B. 62D99 3/5/2; Cudworth, 1891, pp. 249–50; Hustwick, 1962, no. 25.

14. BRADFORD ●
Bradford Tradesmens' Home
At Lilycroft, off Heaton Road, grid ref. SE 135 352. Founded 1875 by Henry Brown, with 1877 additions by Eliza Wright.

Fig. 47 Bradford Tradesmens' Homes. Part of the north range which includes the chapel/reading room with its supporting pair of alpaca. Individual gardens front each house, separated by paths from the central lawn and sitting area. *Photo: author.*

Spacious four-sided rectangular courtyard, broken by corner entrance past secretary's house. Two storey stone houses, graduated green slate roof, overhanging eaves supported by timbering, dormer windows. Tall chimneys, terracotta finials over dormers and on ridge. Reading room/chapel protrudes from one long side as a bay with clock tower, stained glass windows and statues of alpaca beside entrance. Secretary's house modestly Gothic, but overall effect more *cottage ornée*. Central and individual gardens with bootscrapers.

Plaque on long side facing chapel: '1878 this block of houses was built by Eliza Wright and son John Cockshott Wright in memory of Isaac Wright esq. JP and his son Charles Henry Wright'. Foundation stone laid by Titus Salt.

Residents: 42 M/F/C pensioners of the Tradesmen's Benevolent Fund or Spinsters' Endowment Fund, the secretary and resident gardener. Pension. Companions allowed, minimum income.

Refs. CC, ii, pp 156, 165; B.T.B.A., 1915–99.

15. CARLETON-IN-CRAVEN •

Spence's Hospital

On the edge of the village, renamed Spence's Court, grid ref. SD 969 496

Founded 1698 by Ferrand Spence, with later funding 1872 by Agnes Niven.

Small two storey stone courtyard. Upper gallery for access forms timber colonnade below; entry through pillared gateway in high wall. Otherwise unadorned. Bedsit units with communal facilities

Fig. 48 Spence's Hospital, Carleton-in-Craven. The gateway to the secluded courtyard; whilst still almshouses, the renaming suits twentieth-century conventions. *Photo: author.*

Fig. 49 Carlton Almshouses, now known as Stapleton Cottages after the founder Miles Stapleton. The recent restoration plaque indicates the continuing involvement of the landowning family. *Photo: author.*

now warden accommodation. Large garden to rear, rented out. Lengthy inscription records building and renovation. The story is that Ferrand, a London businessman, was lost on the moors and taken in by an elderly woman. He founded the hospital in gratitude, not forgetting his Midland roots.

Residents: 12 F (later M/F), 6 from Carleton, 6 from Market Bosworth. From 1887, matron elected from almswomen. Pension, garden produce.

Refs: CC, ii, pp. 299, 303–7; Naylor, 1992; Pevsner, 1967, p. 157.

16. CARLTON, near Goole •

Carlton Almshouses

Known as Stapleton Cottages, in the village, on the edge of Lord Beaumont's estates, grid ref. SE 648 241.

Founded 1693 by Miles Stapleton, rebuilt 1901.

Small single storey row of red brick and red pantiles. Units of 1 room and lean-to each, unadorned as farm labourers' cottages. Large garden.

Plaque lists family members responsible for rebuild but not foundation.

Residents: 4 M/F, local poor, estate workers. Pension and fuel.

Refs: CC, v, pp. 490, 511–12; HU. DDCA (2) 11/13: DDCA 4/123, 125.

17. CAWOOD

James's Hospital

Founded 1723, rebuilt and extended 1984.

Residents: 4 M/F. Pension.

Refs: CC, v, pp. 102, 117.

18. CAWOOD •

Waterhouse Smith's Hospital

On the old road running east from the village, behind the river embankment, 1/2 mile from [17], grid ref. SE 570 379.

Founded 1839.

Fig. 50 Waterhouse Smith's Hospital, Cawood. This row with its central pediment is undergoing routine maintenance. *Photo: author.*

Single storey brick row, slate roof, stone surrounds to doors and windows. Central pediment capped with stone ball over through passage, otherwise unadorned. Units originally 2 rooms with large fireplace and cupboards. Individual and shared gardens.

Residents: 6 M/F, local. Pension.

Rules include care of gardens, no business or school on premises.

Refs: CC, v, pp. 122–3; Bell, 1987

19. CRIGGLESTONE •

Victoria Memorial, formerly Worrill's Almshouses

Among fields on the back lane, nearer to Pledwick, grid ref. 328 154.

Worrill's foundation was pre-1691, replaced rather than rebuilt in 1901.

Small single storey row, red brick and grey slate, two projecting sections with gablets, wooden bargeboards, overall unadorned. Repaired by township who funded replacement.

Plaques: LHS 'Worrill's 1691 Almshouses', RHS 'Victoria 1901 Memorial'.

Architect; J. Thornton of Wakefield.

Residents: 4 (3) usually F, local. Pension.

Refs: CC, v, pp. 461, 482; Taylor, 1976, pp. 40 -1.

20. DARFIELD

Darfield Almshouses

Founded possibly late 1500s by the Saville family, amalgamated with Maude charity in 1893.

Residents: 4 F or elderly poor M/F, local. Pension.

Refs: CC, i, pp. 76, 82; Jordan, 1961, pp. 262–3.

21. DARNALL

Darnall Almshouses

Samuel Staniforth of Liverpool set up voluntary charity, possibly replacing earlier ruinous almshouse sold in 1859.

Residents: 4 F.

Refs: CC, i, pp. 440, 740.

22. DONCASTER

St. Thomas's Hospital

Founded 1557 by Thomas Ellis at St. Sepulchregate, rebuilt 1737, demolition proposed 1898. 'Two rooms and a garden each'.

Residents: 6 M/F 'fallen into poverty by sickness or misfortune'. Pension, bedding.

Gateway re-erected outside museum on Chequer Road. *(See Figure 95)*

Refs: CC, i, pp. 107, 130–4; DA. DX/War B5, B12; Jackson, 1881, pp. 53–71; Jordan, 1961, p. 261.

23. DONCASTER

Stock's Almshouses, known as Old Almshouses.

Founded c.1621, rebuilt at the Holmes 1860 by the corporation who extended and maintained them.

Residents: 3, later 7 M/F. Pension from other charities.

Refs: CC, i, pp. 109, 135–7; Jackson, 1881, p. 72–6; Jordan, 1961, p. 273.

24. DONCASTER •

Tomlinson Charity

On Elmfield Road among contemporary terraced housing, grid ref. SE 580 026.

Founded 1894 by George and Anne Clay in memory of Anne's brother John Tomlinson.

Long two storey row of 12 units. Brick and slate, unadorned but with stepped brick porches. Lower two-light sash windows with semi-dormers above.

Fig. 52 Tomlinson's Charity, Doncaster: a long brick row contained in a residential street. *Photo: author.*

Fig. 51 St. Thomas's Hospital, Doncaster. a) (*Left*) White's engraving of the unadorned two storey building of 1737. The gateway was probably preserved from an earlier phase. b) (*Right*) Two alternative estimates were offered for rebuilding in the 1730s. The mention of 'old and new buildings' suggests previous rebuilds. The trustees chose the more expensive option of 'six rooms below and six above'. *C. Jackson, 1881, Doncaster Charities, published by White (a); Doncaster Archive, DX War. B5 (b).*

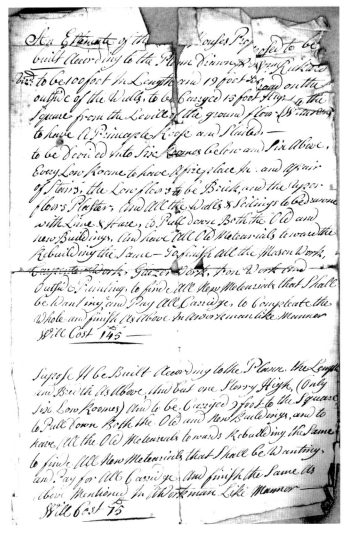

Pair of plaques: 'Tomlinson Charity 1894' set into boundary wall.
Residents: 12 M/F, local.
Refs. Doncaster Gazette Directories, 1900–10; Neeves, M. (letter, 2 June 2005).

25. DRAX, near Goole

Read's Free School and Almshouse
On Town Street at the edge of the village, grid ref. SE 677 267.
Founded 1669 by Richard Read.
Closed and converted to outpensions 1893; school rebuilt late nineteenth century incorporates former plaque.
Residents: 3 M + 3 F, scholars as lodgers. Pension, uniform. Prayers in schoolroom.
Refs: CC, v, pp. 112–24; ER. DDCL/560; WYAS,L. GA/A/9; Baines, 1822, p. 492.

26. EARBY

Crowther's charity
Founded 1874.
Part of a row of cottages.
Residents: 3 F, local. Pension.
Refs: CC, ii, pp. 805–7.

27. ECCLESFIELD

Bamforth's Almshouses
Founded 1730, at Wadsley Bridge.
No endowment, maintained by parish.
Residents: 3 from Owlerton, 3 from Ecclesfield.
Refs; CC, i, pp. 154, 176.

28. ECCLESFIELD

Barnes Hall Hospital
On the edge of the founder's estste, south of Burncross, grid ref. SK 338 955.

Founded 1630, built 1639 by founder's brother.
Only the plaque remains, in a modern wall beside the lodge.
Residents: 6, tenants first choice. Pension, fuel and vegetable garden.
Refs: CC, i, pp. 153, 174.

29. ECCLESFIELD
Sylvester's Hospital
At Mortomley Lane End.
Founded 1693, additional endowment 1801 from Ann Reresby.
Residents: 6 M/F, preferably from northern part of parish. Small pension.
Refs: CC, i, pp. 153, 175.

30. FEATHERSTONE
Bead House
Founded 1613 by John Hamerton, funded by the Frank family from Pontefract, later by the parish.
Residents: 3 M/F, local. Very small pension.
Bell in roof of cottage to be rung by almsman when a funeral came from Purston Jaglin to the nearby churchyard.
Refs: CC, v, pp. 146, 149–51.

31. FERRYBRIDGE
Clarkson's Charity
Founded 1699, maintained by the parish.
Residents: 4 F, local. Small pension.
Refs: CC, v, pp. 170, 176.

32. FLOCKTON •
Carter's Almshouses

Fig. 53 Carter's Almshouses, Flockton. Detail of doorway. *Photo: author.*

On Chapel Street, inset into the churchyard, opposite the original site with the school, grid ref. SE 241 149.
Founded 1698, rebuilt 1868, now empty.
Brick and slate pair of cottages, unadorned save for stone quoins and decorative bargeboards.
Originally intended as 2 sharing, each unit 1 room and lean-to.
Plaques: 'Dono Ricardi Carter de Flockton 1697', 'Rebuilt 1868'.
Residents: 2 M/F, local. Pension.
Refs: CC, iii, pp. 942–9; Gavaghan, E. (letter, 3 July 2002).

33. GAWBER, near Barnsley
Barber's Almshouses
On Wood View Lane, originally beside the school.
Founded before 1715 by Martha Adams, formerly Barber.
Residents: 2F. Pension, fuel.
Refs: CC, v, pp. 98, 106–9, BA. BB22/1–8; Bretton, undated, pp. 51–4; Wilkinson, c.1869.

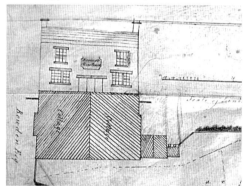

Fig. 54 Barber's Almshouses, Gawber.
Location of the almshouses and their land (map undated). *Barnsley Archive and Library Service, BB 22/1–8.*

34. GRINDLETON, near Clitheroe •
Mary Brown's Almshouses

Fig. 55 Mary Brown's Almshouses, Grindleton.
One of the enclosed porches, on the west end of the row which faces south across the valley. *Photo: author.*

On Sawley Road, just outside the village, grid ref. SD 765 458.
Founded 1860.
Single storey row, symmetrical with three front-facing gables, projecting central unit and porches at ends. Low pitched stone roof with graduated slates and stone kneelers. Unadorned with Gothic touches. Set back behind wall, facing away from road across fields to the Ribble; small garden each and drying ground.
Plaque: 'This hospital was built and endowed by Mary Brown of Rathmell in remembrance of her brothers and sisters AD 1860'.
Residents: 8 (10) F, 60+, local. Pension.
Rules include prayers to be read twice weekly by the vicar.
Refs: CC, ii, pp. 385, 573.

35. HALIFAX •

John Abbott's Trustees Ladies' Homes

On Skircoat Green Road, grid ref. SE 085 245.
Founded 1886.
Small stone semi-detached houses with 2 detached, Gothic, set out in a circular layout in gardens. Units each one up, one down with room for maid.

Residents: 10 F, local, in reduced circumstances; porter. Pension, minimum income.
Refs: CC, iii, pp. 353–9; WYAS,C. HX FW34/41–48; HX Misc.703/15; NOR 20/1,2; Halifax Courier,1965.

36. HALIFAX •

Frank (Francis) Crossley's Almshouses

On Margaret Street, off Hopwood Lane, backing onto the founder's mansion, grid ref. SE 088 249.
Founded 1855.
Long two storey stone row with slate roof. Each end

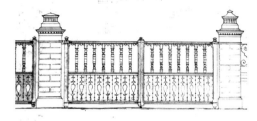

Fig. 56 John Abbott's Trustees Ladies' Homes, Halifax. a) Architect's drawing for a respectable but unostentatious gateway allowing carriage access. b) The porter's lodge. c) One of the semi-detached pairs with upstairs accommodation for the maid. *WYAS,C Misc. 703/15 (a); photos: author (b and c).*

Fig. 57 Frank Crossley's Almshouses, Halifax. a) View along the row, from one of the protruding bays to the terminal turret. b) The founder's own family home, with its chateau architecture in contrast to the Gothic almshouses, which are at right angles, immediately to the right of the photo. *Photos: author.*

finished by a tower at right angles, with additional crenellated storey and oriel windows in gables either side. Gothic but lacks presence in enclosed situation. Strip garden.

Initials 'FC 1855' and scroll 'Of thine own have we given thee' on tower.

Residents: 22 M/F/C, local, usually nonconformist. Porter appointed from residents. Pension.

Refs: CC, iii, pp. 108–113; WYAS,C. HX 298, 666; H Misc.129; Bretton, 1953, pp. 65–67; Halifax Courier, 1965; Pevsner, 1967, p. 237.

37. HALIFAX •
Joseph Crossley's Almshouses
On Arden Road, grid ref. SE 087 248.

Founded 1863 and completed 1870 by Joseph's son Edward.

Large three-sided courtyard, asymmetrical to fit site, two phases unified. Two storey stone decorated with numerous gables and turrets; central tower originally containing boardroom with adjacent campanile; chapel in longer side

above accommodation. Some two storey units, some bedsits. Extremely Gothic with French chateau style roofs. Central garden.

Architect: Roger Ives of Halifax.

Residents: 48 M/F/C, local, usually nonconformist. Pension, furniture, founder's day outing.

Refs: CC, iii, pp. 113–122; TC; Bretton, 1953, pp. 90–91; Girouard, 1970; Halifax Courier, 1965; Pevsner, 1967, p. 236.

38. HALIFAX
Hopkinson Crowther Almshouses
Founded 1613 by sisters Jane and Ellen, rebuilt 1748 and bought by Waterhouse charity mid-nineteenth century.

In town centre near parish church, associated with school and giving lodgings to scholars.

Residents: 18 F and schoolmaster, later 21 with 3 more units for school. Pension paid by parish, clothing.

Refs: CC, iii, pp. 233, 433; WYAS,C. HX T626, 627; Misc.137/66–91; NOR 19.

Fig. 58 Joseph Crossley's Almshouses, Halifax. a) Architect's drawing for the north wing, signed and dated R. Ives, 1867. A flap (towards the right) offered an alternative; pencil notes reflect discussion with the client. Ultimately the turret was omitted and the less ornate version agreed. b) This section through the north range shows the internal arrangements, with the end unit, turned at right angles, providing a visual stop. c) The north range as built. d) The tower at the centre of the west range originally contained the boardroom, now warden's accommodation. *Trustee Collection (a and b); photos: author (c and d).*

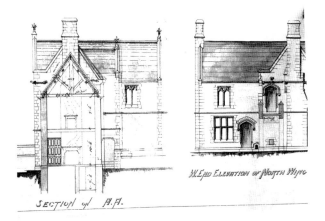

SECTION on A.A.

W. End Elevation of North Wing

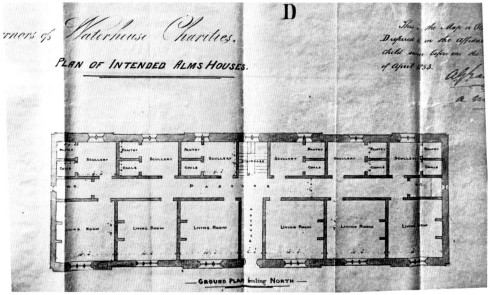

Fig. 59 Nathaniel Waterhouse Charity, Halifax. Architect's proposal from Charles Child of Halifax in 1853 for a replacement self-contained block of almshouses with modern conveniences. Each unit would be entered from the central spine, but making a meal would involve crossing this communal passage. *WYAS,C Misc. 137/22.*

39. HALIFAX
Nathaniel Waterhouse Charity, now Waterhouse Homes

On Harrison Road since 1848, grid ref. SE 085 257.

Founded 1642, rebuilt 1812, 1848 new site, rebuilt again 1967.

Formerly in two wings of large Gothic complex with Bluecoat School. Surrounding garden.

Residents: 10 M/F, from 10 townships. Pension, clothing.

Refs: CC, iii, pp. 225–30; WYAS,C. HAS 672/42–49; HX 96a/2, 3, 4; Misc. 137/18–65, 66 91; Clayton, 1940; Halifax Courier, 1967; Jordan, 1961, p. 276; Pevsner, 1967, p. 233; Watson, 1775.

40. HARROGATE •
Rogers' Almshouses

Now called Rogers' Square on Belford Road, grid ref. SE 304 509.

Founded 1868 by a Bradford businessman who retired to Harrogate.

Stone courtyard, partly single, partly two storey, central clock tower, symmetrically placed gables, graduated green slate roof. Two-light mullioned

Fig. 60 Rogers' Almshouses, Harrogate. a) The two storey north range has gablets and a unifying string course. b) The dominant tower in the central range has a clock facing all four directions to benefit the town. *Photos: author.*

windows, plain below, Gothic above, with an ornamental window (possibly former door) in tower with beehive motif. Finials on gables and tower, working clock face on three sides. Formal garden and low front wall with railing. In the 1870s and '80s an enclave was formed with school, cottage hospital and nurses' home.

Modern plaque explains beehive emblem for industry and 1992 refurbishment.

Residents: 12 M/F, Bradford and Harrogate, preferably tradespeople in reduced circumstances.

Refs: Yorkshire Post, 1968.

41. HEMSWORTH •
Archbishop Holgate's Hospital

Among trees on Robin Lane, at the outskirts of Hemsworth, grid ref. SE 411 125.

Founded 1555, rebuilt 1770 and 1858.

Two long single storey rows, red brick banded with blue, patterned slate roof. Angular and curved bays, stepped gables, paired porches, stone sills, lintels and door heads. Central gateway through front row, flanked by porter's house and boardroom, aligned with chapel in rear row. Two additional units added to match, 1914. Extensive gardens; separate master's house in similar style with more Gothic detail. Previous building plain stone row behind parish church.

Architect: Robert Pope of London.

Residents: 20 M/F, local. Pension, fuel, clothing; originally uniform and communal dining. Master (cleric) and porter and matron (from 1860).

Refs: CC, v, pp. 217–19, 223–32; WYAS,W. C345 1/1–6, 17, 26, 43; C345 3/1; WYAS,Y. DD58; Baines, 1822, p. 523; Banks, 1871, pp. 324–29; Hewitt, 1862 pp. 154, 158; Taylor, 1976, pp. 46–7; Pevsner, 1967, p. 261.

Fig. 61 Archbishop Holgate's Hospital, Hemsworth. a) Part of the upper row which has both pointed and curved bays, and inset porches with access to the units either side. b) The chapel forms the central feature of the upper row, continuing the banded brickwork and further dignified by additional stonework and a belltower. c) The gatehouse forms the imposing centre of the lower row, housing the boardroom and (formerly) the porter and matron and their family. d) The boardroom containing the fittings designed for it in 1860. *Photos: author.*

Fig. 62 Holmfirth Monumental Almshouses. View looking up from the road with the gateway to the steps in the foreground. *Photo: author.*

42. HOLMFIRTH •

Holmfirth Monumental Almshouses

On the outskirts, above the road to New Mill (A635), grid ref. SE 148 090.

Founded 1860 by public subscription to a disaster fund after Bilberry Reservoir flooded in 1852; a further £1,000 from local fund-raising.

Two storey stone row enhanced with wings, central gabled tower, steeply pitched decorative slate roof. Lancet windows, fleur de lys motif and leaf moulding on terminals; very Gothic. Entry through Gothic arch, up steep flights of steps with small terraced garden.

Plaque over arch lists 14 trustees representing 7 townships, donor of the land Cookson Stephens, and architect William Hill.

Residents: 5 M/F, local. Pension.

Refs: CC, iii, pp. 795–8;WYAS,K. WYK 1086 1/1–6; WYAS 263; Sykes, 1910.

43. HOOK, near Goole

Jefferson's Almshouses

On Water Lane, off main street and behind river embankment, grid ref. SE 762 255.

Founded before 1721, rebuilt 1854, replaced late twentieth century.

Originally included unit for school, taken over by parish for poor couple; may have been linked with poors' house.

Residents: 3 'oldest and poorest', local. Pension, gardens.

Refs: CC, v, pp. 490, 511–12.

44. HORBURY •

St. Leonard's Hospital, formerly Wormald's

On Tithebarn Street, near old school and lock-up, off the square with St. Peter and St. Leonard's Church by John Carr, grid ref. SE 295 185.

Founded 1731, rebuilt 1888 by the township for £600 from public subscription and renamed.

Simple and symmetrical single storey stone row with gables, slate roof and tall chimneys. Rear wing for community nurse. Garden strip.

Plaque: 'This hospital has been erected to the glory of God, for the relief of the poor of Horbury and in memory of the jubilee of our gracious Queen Victoria and was dedicated by William Walsham first bishop of Wakefield. 1888'.

Residents: 4 'aged paupers', local. No pension.

Refs: CC, v, pp. 588–9, 714.

Fig. 63 St. Leonard's Hospital (Wormald's), Horbury. The simple stone row carries the street name, St. Leonard's Yard. The nurse's house is tucked behind. *Photo: author.*

Fig. 64 Thomas Holroyd endowed four existing cottages to form his almshouse in Huddersfield. *Photo: author.*

Fig. 65 Popples Almshouses at Illingworth: a) set back from the road and at right angles to the school with a plot of land behind; b) windows and doors show recent renovation to the stonework. *Ordnance Survey, Sheet 17, 1892 (a); photo: author (b).*

45. HUDDERSFIELD
Hall's Charity
At Booth Town.
Founded 1687, demolished 1876. Linked to school.
Residents: 3 M + 3 F, local. Pension and outpensioners.
Refs: CC, iii, pp. 456–60; Huddersfield archive H Misc.362, SC 13/143.

46. HUDDERSFIELD •
Holroyd's Almshouses
At Birkby Fold, off Birkby Lodge Road, grid ref. SE 135 182.
Founded 1830, additional endowment 1880 from J. Armitage.
Row of two storey stone cottages, not purpose-built. Small garden, no space to rear.
Plaque: 'Holroyd's Almshouse 1830'.
Residents: 4 M/F, local. No pension.
Refs: CC, iii, pp. 678–70; WYAS,K. KC 627 3/1; S/HC Box 115/6/7, 11, 12.

47. ILLINGWORTH •
Wadsworth's or Popples Almshouses
Off School Lane, beyond former National School and farm, grid ref. SE 077 293.
Founded 1832 by Elizabeth Wadsworth and built 1840.
Single storey stone row of 6 units, each one room and lean-to. Three-light mullioned windows beneath drip moulds; central pediment with finials. Stone slate roof. Small garden to front, originally almshouse field to rear.
Plaque: 'These 6 almshouses for poor women of Holdsworth, widows or if unmarried not less than 50 years of age, were erected by the Trustees of Popples Charity pursuant to the directions of the benevolent foundress the late Mrs. Elizabeth Wadsworth of Holdsworth House AD 1840. 'For when the ear heard her, then it blessed her, and when the eye saw her it gave witness unto her, Job xxix, vii".
Residents: 6 F, local. Pension. Supervised by schoolmaster; church attendance required.
Refs: CC, iii, pp. 442–7; Halifax Courier, 1965.

48. KEXBOROUGH, near Barnsley
Robert Thickett's Donation
Founded 1771, built 1780.
Plaque (now lost) 'These houses were built by the donation of Robert Thickett in the year 1780 and are to be occupied by poor widows whom the town shall appoint'. It is said that Robert's mother was blind, and in gratitude for the relief that she received he made this gift to the township. They maintained the premises, but also used them for families.
Residents: 2 M/F, local.
Refs; CC, v, pp. 97, 105; Wilkinson, c.1869, pp. 104, 107.

Fig. 66 The Leathley Almshouses of 1769: a) the row; b) the central unit, formerly the schoolhouse. *Photos: author.*

49. KIRKTHORPE •
Frieston Hospital
On Half Moon Lane in the old village, grid ref. SE 361 210.
Founded 1595.
Single storey, nearly square, stone with central hipped stone slate roof and single massive chimney. Mullioned windows, restored. Inside, 6 small rooms and 1 slightly larger lead off a central hall, with fireside seating. Unadorned, but with quality timbering in hall. Large garden, originally including matron's house.
Plaque (replacement) 'John Frieston of Altofts, esquire, founded and endowed this Hospital AD 1595. He that hath mercy on the poor, happy is he Prov. 14.21'.
Residents: 7 M, one designated senior brother, 1 F. Pension, possibly milk and produce.
Now a private house.
Refs: CC, v, pp. 720–4, 728–34; TC; WYAS,W. C493/15, 37, 67–70; C547 2/5/11; C547 4/1/1, 5; D75/91; WYAS,Y. DD154; Anon., 2000; Banks, 1871, pp. 238, 259–61; Everett, undated; Hewitt, 1862, pp. 160–1; Pevsner, 1967, p. 294; Taylor, 1976, pp. 48–9.

50. KIRKTHORPE
Sagar's Hospital
Between Frieston Hospital and the river, grid ref. SE 360 211.
Founded 1558 by Othoneus Sagar, rebuilt 1766, demolished 1940s.
Seen by the local community in parallel with Frieston, and maintained by them. Charities now amalgamated.
Residents: 4 F, local. Pension, fuel.
refs: CC, v, pp. 720, 728; WYAS,W. D75/91; Banks, 1871, pp. 256–59.

51. KNARESBOROUGH
Garth's Almshouses
On Briggate.
Original founder unknown. Richard Davison, 1884, gave two groups of cottages to the town, half to be rented, half rent-free.
Residents: 6 M/F.
Refs: CC, iv, p. 282.

52. LEATHLEY, near Otley •
Leathley Almshouses
On raised ground opposite the church, looking across the flood plain to the hills, grid ref. SE 232 471.
Founded 1769 by Ann Hitch on behalf of her brother.
Single storey stone row with stone slate roof, unadorned save for the central semi-circular window. Central projecting block was originally schoolroom which moved to building to rear, now village hall. Small garden.
Plaque: 'Fulfilling to the utmost of her ability the benevolent intentions of Henry Hitch esq. This school and hospital were erected and endowed by Ann Hitch, the only surviving sister and executrix 1769'.
Residents: 4 M/F. Pension.
Refs: CC, iv, pp. 291, 293; Fletcher, 1900, p. 122; Pevsner, 1967, p. 302; Speight, 1900.

Fig. 67 At Sir John Lewis's Hospital, Ledsham, the narrow path gives access to each home through its modern porch, while a lawn extends to the right of the photo. *Photo: author.*

53. LEDSHAM •
Sir John's Hospital, now Cottages

Behind the church and Lady Betty Hastings' orphanage and girls' school in the village centre, grid ref. SE 456 298.

Founded 1670 by Sir John Lewis.

Two storey stone row with stone slate roof, facing south. Mullioned two-light windows, upstairs tucked under the eaves, below attached to a string course. No central features, unadorned. Large garden.

Residents: 11 M/F, in 'reduced circumstances'. Pension, fuel, clothing.

Refs: CC, v, pp. 265–6, 275–6; Pevsner, 1967, p. 304.

54. LEEDS
Gott's Charity

Foundation date uncertain; 1880 addition by daughter Harriet Gott.

On Chapel Lane, Armley, 6 units with a school.

Residents: 12 F. Pension.

Converted to private housing, 1960s.

Refs: CC, iv, p. 464–5; www.leodis.net.

55. LEEDS •
Harrison's Hospital

On Raglan Road, Woodhouse, grid ref. SE 288 356.

Founded 1653 by John Harrison beside St. John's Church, rebuilt 1849 on new site. Additional endowments 1751 from Catherine Parker, 1759 from Josiah Midgley and 1792 from Arthur Ikin.

Large two storey courtyard, red brick with stone facings and slate roof. Symmetrical façade with corner gables; entrance through tower with bay window and battlements. Individual doors off courtyard garden, but inner face plainer than outer. Slope gives feeling of height and enclosure.

Residents: 52 F, local. Pension, bedstead and annual dinner. Chapel till 1726. Porter or matron. Amalgamated with Mary Potter's Charity [59].

Refs; CC, iv, pp. 301, 368–72; WYAS,L. GA/2/26; Baines, 1822, p. 27; Douglas and Powell, 1993; Kelly, vol. ii, 1904, p. 23; www.leodis.net.

Fig. 68 Harrison's Hospital, Leeds. External view of the former almshouses bounded by Mark Lane and Wade Lane with St. John's Church, also founded by John Harrison, in the background. The building to the right functioned as a school, replacing the earlier almshouse chapel, and is now used by Age Concern. *Leeds Library and Information Service, 20021017–86935062.*

Fig. 69 Stephen Nicholson's Almshouses at Roundhay, Leeds. The central unit is again used as a school within the row of six, which retains its graduated slate roof but with chimneys much reduced as gas replaced solid fuel. *Photo: author.*

56. LEEDS
Holbeck Almshouse
Founded 1835 by Tobias Isles from the Explosion Fund raised by public subscription. Condemned and due to be rebuilt 1892.
Residents: 4.
Refs: CC, iv, pp. 502–3.

57. LEEDS
Jenkinson's Hospital
Founded 1643, rebuilt on St. Mark's Road, Woodhouse 1806 and 1838.
Additional funding from Dalley's Charity 1823.
Residents: 8/9 M/F. Pension, with more for eldest. Ex-miners and widows first choice.
Refs: CC, iv, pp. 300, 373; Baines, 1822, p. 27; www. leodis.net.

58. LEEDS •
Stephen Nicholson's Almshouses
On Wetherby Road, Roundhay, grid ref. SE 337 372.
Founded 1837 where already built; linked to school.
Single storey stone row, graduated slate roof. Central block with projecting porch, decorative barge boards on end gables. Simple hood moulds to doors and windows. Raised above road in front of St. John's Church.
Residents: 6 M/F, old servants first choice. Pension. Church attendance.
Now Church Cottages and Leeds Montessori School.
Refs: CC, iv, pp. 58–61; www.leodis.net.

59. LEEDS •
Mary Potter's Hospital
Now on Raglan Road with Harrison's [55].
Founded 1728, built 1736 at Wade Lane, rebuilt 1852 on St. Columba's Street, Woodhouse.
Residents: 10 F, from Leeds, Wakefield or York. Pension.
Refs: CC, iv, pp. 305, 374; WYAS,L. uncatalogued; Baines, 1822, p. 27; Kelly, vol. ii, 1904, p. 23.

Fig. 70 Mary Potter's Hospital, Leeds: inside the courtyard of the present Harrison Potter Almshouses. The crenellated entrance tower may be deliberately evocative of that in the old Harrison's Hospital. *Photo: author.*

Fig. 71 Fountain's Hospital, Linton: a) the inturned row of the front façade; b) the less public, and extended, side range is far less imposing than the front to the village green. *Photos: author.*

60. LEEDS •

John Scott's Almshouses

Founded 1891, built 1896 on Middleton Road, Hunslet, grid ref. SE 315 304.

Two-storey ranges about a courtyard. Brick with heavy stone facings, gablets and finials. Porches with stone columns; false balcony at first floor level.

Bust of founder on plinth in centre of garden.

Plaques: 'Erected and endowed by John Scott Esq. AD 1896'; named trustees, architect John E. Leake.

Residents: 10 M/F, tradespeople, poor widows. Pension.

Refs: CC, iv, pp. 514–15; Kelly, 1904, p. 23.

61. LEEDS •

Martha Walker's Almshouses

On Church Road, Armley, next to the clinic, grid ref. SE 273 335.

Founded 1883.

Two storey stone row with protruding centre, gabled and Gothic.

Plaque 'These almshouses were erected by Martha Walker, Nancroft House, Armley, in memory of her parents, brothers and sister, AD 1883'.

Residents: 6.

No further information.

62. LINTON, near Grassington •

Fountain's Hospital

Facing village green, stream to one side, cluster of cottages to the other; grid ref. SD 998 640.

Founded 1721 by Richard Fountain.

Imposing two storey row with extended wings and central tower with Venetian window, cupola and urns. Rear wings added 1892. Quality dressed stone and elaborate quoins on front façade. Interior includes chapel, library and passage to garden. Paved area at front.

Fountain supplied timber to Vanbrugh, who at least influenced the design.

Residents: 6, later 8, M/F, local. Pension, clothing. Minister to read prayers, administration by agent. Rules include cleaning and church attendance.

Refs; CC, ii, pp. 517, 522; Banks, 1862, pp. 36 -7; Pevsner, 1967, p. 353; Whitaker, 1973, pp. 550–2.

63. LONG PRESTON •

Long Preston Hospital

Just outside the village, beside the railway, grid ref. SD 838 577.

Founded 1613 by James Knowles, rebuilt 1859.

Single storey stone row with graduated slates and tall tapering chimneys. Central unit contains chapel (now accommodation). Mullioned three-

Fig. 72 Long Preston Hospital. a) The long row has paired doors and three-light windows. The higher roof of the central block (on the right) indicates the former chapel. b) The head of the redundant chapel window ornaments the almshouse garden. *Photos: author.*

Fig. 73 Methley: a long row of three with external chimney stack and graduated slate roof. *Photo: author.*

light windows; unadorned. Small gardens.
Residents: 10 M/F, local. Pension from Smith's Charity 1732, fuel. Visiting reader.
Rules include chapel attendance and wearing uniform.
Refs: CC, ii, pp. 537, 543; NY. PR/PRL 18/8/17–19, 24; PR/PRL 18/9/4–7.

64. METHLEY, near Rothwell •
Methley Almshouses
At Woodend by Almshouses Wood, on the edge of the former Methley Hall estate, grid ref. SE 378 270.
Founded c. 1700 by the Savile family.
Low single storey row of 3 units, one room each. Stone with graduated stone slate roof. Two-light mullioned windows either side of doors with long and short work and heavy flattened arch lintels. External chimney stacks to gable ends.Forms one side of hamlet behind open garden.
Residents: 8, later 3 F, estate workers.
Five demolished in 1920s, remainder now private houses.
Refs: Minett, undated.

65. MEXBOROUGH
The Hospital Houses
Founded 1728 by William Calverley, attributed to William Horne of Wakefield. Demolished 1910 for road widening.
Residents: 6 F.
Refs: CC, i, pp. 304, 307; BA. D2 MD542/1.

66. MONK BRETTON, near Barnsley
Talbot's Almshouses
At Burton Grange, north of the water mill, grid ref. SE 372 065.
Founded 1654 by Dame Maria Talbot, daughter of the Earl of Shrewsbury and widow of William Airmyn.

Residents: 6 F, local. Pension, possibly clothing.
Refs: CC, i, pp. 424, 446; BA. BM 2/1; Banks, 1871, p. 360; Barnsley Civic Review, 1955, no. 78, p. 2.

67. OTLEY
Fawkes's Charity
Presumably a medieval foundation; also known as the Leper House.
Residents: 3 F. Pension.
Refs: CC, iv, p. 604.

68. PLEDWICK •
Harrison's Homes for the Aged Poor
Above the Wakefield road, near Newmillerdam, grid ref. SE 333 163.
Founded 1885.
Three pairs of semis in a row; stone with a rustic look but dressed on bays and pediments, gablets on side walls; eclectic detail. Bedsit accommodation, described by CC as 'picturesque and superior'. Ground rises to rear, no visible garden.
Plaque on central house 'Harrison's Homes for the Aged Poor, [---] builder, erected 1885 by Samuel F Harrison, Fred. Simpson Architect'.
Residents: 6 M/F, local 'deserving poor'. Pension.
Refs: CC, v, pp. 479–81.

69. PONTEFRACT
Bede House
On Micklegate.
Medieval foundation, rebuilt 1671 and 1890. Additional endowment 1722 by Catherine Favell.
Residents: 8 M + 8 F; by 1811 only 2, the rest replaced by a workhouse.
Refs: CC, v, p. 337; Boothroyd, 1807; Fox, 1827, p. 297.

70. PONTEFRACT •
Cowper's Hospital
Founded 1668 near Beast Fair, rebuilt 1765 at the Butts for £90. Rebuilt again 1888.

Residents: 4 F. Pension.
Now privately occupied.
Refs: CC, v, pp. 338–9; Fox, 1827, p. 297.

71. PONTEFRACT
Matthew Frank's Hospital
Founded about 1650 on Micklegate, possibly on site of former Lazar House.
Residents: 2 F.
Refs: CC, v, pp. 339, 358; Fox, 1827, pp. 296, 327.

72. PONTEFRACT
Robert Frank's Hospital
On Micklegate, next to [69].
Founded 1737, repaired by parish.
Residents: 2.
Refs: CC, v, p. 358; Fox, 1827, pp. 329–30.

73. PONTEFRACT
Almshouse and College of Sir Robert Knolles, known as Trinities
Founded about 1385 on Micklegate; Robert's wife Constance came from Pontefract. Rebuilt 1859, supported by the corporation.
Described by Fox as a 'square entered through a wooden gatehouse' to a 'church, hall and many mansions for the poor'. The large common room and separate sleeping rooms were replaced in 1859 by separate wings for M and F, each with a common room.
Residents: 7 M + 7 F and 2 servants. Pension, fuel.
Rules originally required residents to provide a bed, towel, pewter doubler and porringer or cash equivalent, to attend chapel twice daily, and to provide bread and ale on arrival and funeral.
Refs: CC, v, pp. 336–7, 354–6, 365; Cullum, 1989, pp. 346, 354–5; Fox, 1827, pp. 317–27; VCH, 1913, pp. 318–9.

74. PONTEFRACT
Perfect's Hospital
Founded 1767 by Alderman Perfect (who also repaired other almshouses) on Micklegate, financed by liquorice and run by the corporation.
Residents: 3 C. A widow or widower might move on to Knolles.
Refs: CC, v, p. 337; Fox, Fox, 1827, p. 327.

75. PONTEFRACT
College and Hospital of St. Nicholas
Medieval foundation taken on by the corporation; royal charter 1605. Rebuilt 1890.
Plaque 'builded by Thomas Sayle of Pontefract, tallow chandler, deceased 1673'.
Residents: 13 including 2 servants. Parish pension, fuel.
Refs: CC, v, pp. 334–6, 353–4; Fox, 1827, pp. 313–17; VCH, 1913, p. 319.

76. PONTEFRACT
Thwaite's Hospital
On Newgate at Tanshelf.
Founded 1620, rebuilt 1863. Demolished 1960s.
Residents: 4 F, 'ancient poor women of good years', local. Pension, fuel, garden produce.
Refs: CC, v, p. 338; Fox, 1827, pp. 330–1.

77. PONTEFRACT
Ward's Hospital
On Front Street at Tanshelf.
Founded 1520s or 1550s, rebuilt at uncertain date.
Residents: 2 F. Small pension.
Refs: CC, v, pp. 344, 405–7.

78. PONTEFRACT
Watkinson's Hospital
On Northgate.
Founded 1765, built by 1778, from the estate of Dr. Watkinson of Ackworth. 'Far the best of the almshouses in Pontefract', according to CC.
Residents: 2 F + 2 M from Pontefract with 2 F + 2 M from Ackworth and 1 servant.
Plaque survives in Pontefract Museum.
Refs: CC, v, pp. 340–1, 366; Fox, 1827, p. 344.
N.B. In 1884 all the Pontefract (excluding Tanshelf) almshouse charities were amalgamated and are still run jointly.
Ref. West Yorkshire Archaeology Service, undated (see Fig. 7).

79. RAWMARSH
Goodwin's Charity
Founded 1743, rebuilt 1894. Demolished 1960s.
Terraced in 2 rows above the Swinton to Rotherham road.
Residents: 6 F, local. Pension, fuel.
Refs: CC, i, pp. 349–51.

80. RIPON •
St. Anne's Hospital, also called Maison Dieu
On High St. Agnesgate, grid ref: SE 313 710.
Medieval foundation, refounded in 1623 by the corporation, rebuilt in 1869 and still a municipal charity.
Back-to-back single storey row, brick with decorative brick bands unifying windows and eaves, substantial stone facings and buttresses on both Gothic façades. Chimneys use unusual double ellipse. Single room with bed recess in each unit. Small garden abutting ruined chapel.
Residents: 4 M + 4 F. Pension.
Refs: CC, iv, pp. 599, 646; NY. DC/RIC ix 2/5/9–13; Pearson, 1972, pp. 44–46; Pevsner, 1967, p. 413; VCH, 1913, pp. 329–30.

Fig. 74 St. John's Hospital, Ripon: a) the avenue leading to the almshouses; b) the winged row, in a spacious setting between river and church, but within an urban area. *Photos: author.*

81. **RIPON** •
St. John's Hospital
On Bondgate, beside the river at the edge of the city, grid ref. SE 314 710.

Founded about 1110, survived the Reformation and its master's involvement in the Rising of the North and amalgamated with St. Mary Magdalene in the care of the Dean of Ripon Minster in the 1670s. Rebuilt 1878 in the precinct of St. John's church.

Single storey brick row with wings; single decorative course of blue brick, half-timbered porches and tiled roof. Doors, windows and chimneys mildly Gothic. Large garden.

Residents: originally 2 F, increased to 6.

Refs: CC, iv, pp. 617, 658; NY. DC/RIC ix 6/1; Cullum, 1989; Pearson, 1972, pp. 36–43; VCH, 1913, pp. 327–9.

82. **RIPON** •
Hospital of St. Mary Magdalene
Off Magdalen's Road, beside the river, grid ref. SE 315 717.

Founded about 1115 by Thurstan, Archbishop of York, possibly in two buildings as a leper hospital and staff accommodation. Rebuilt 1674 by Dean Hooke, who established the Minster connection, and rebuilt, still in two parts, 1875 and 1890.

Earlier row, single storey brick with stone lintels, wooden porches and tall chimneys. Each unit forms a small bedsit with lean-to. Unkept grounds and redundant church.

Later row, stone, terminating in a lodge by the road, more substantial porches, emblem of bishop's mitre, and more Gothic than its neighbour. Original leper chapel, restored, to rear.

Residents: 6 + 6. Pension.

Refs: CC, iv, pp. 615, 617; NY. DC/RIC ix 6/1; RL. Y/362 900; Cullum, 1989; Pearson, 1972, pp. 36–43; Pevsner, 1967, p. 413; VCH, 1913, pp. 323–7.

Fig. 75 Hospital of St. Mary Magdalene, Ripon. a) The north row was rebuilt in unadorned brick with tall chimneys in 1875. b) The south row was built in stone in 1890, beside the former leper chapel (on the left, beyond the photo). *Photos: author.*

Fig. 76 Mary Bellamy's Almshouses, Rotherham: a) the neat and simple row with popular gables and three-light windows, as rebuilt in 1897; b) the heavy stone door surround, possibly retained from the previous building, beneath the half-timbered gable. *Photos: author.*

Built 1868 as part of the model town.

Single storey stone buildings interspersed with two storey accommodation for couples. Paired porches and window bays in the Italianate style of Saltaire. Most of the houses form an open courtyard about a public green, the rest across the road adjoining the Infirmary. Porches contain record of names and ages of former, long-lived, residents.

Residents: 45, later 22, M/F/C, local. Pension.

Refs: CC, ii, p. 226; WYAS,B. 29D 87/71; Reynolds, 1983, p. 278.

83. ROTHERHAM •

Mary Bellamy's Almshouses

Off Broome Road at the end of Wellgate, grid ref. SK 435 924.

Founded 1781, rebuilt 1850 and 1897.

Small brick row with tiled roof; large half-timbered and gabled porches, original studded doors, stone buttresses. Small garden, cut off by later development.

Plaques: 'Founded AD 1781' and 'Rebuilt AD 1897'; escutcheon with initial 'B'.

Residents: 4 F. Pension.

Rules include: no male lodgers, keep home clean, care for one another.

Refs: CC, i, pp. 378, 401–3; RALS. 167/T1/1; 167/T2/1.

84. SALTAIRE •

Salt Hospital

On the southern section of Victoria Road, associated with the Infirmary and dispensary, grid ref. SE 139 377.

Fig. 77 The Salt Hospital, Saltaire: a) the end of the long range with a single storey and two storey units sharing an Italianate porch; b) the central feature incorporating the founder's initials below the belltower. *Photos: author.*

Fig. 78 The Widows' Hospital at Sedbergh. The distinctive features are the striped stonework and deep overhang of the roof above the paired hood moulds. Alternate doors have been converted to windows as internal expansion has reduced the number of units. *Photo: J. Hall.*

85. SANDAL, near Wakefield

Grice's and Dickenson's Almshouses, known as Zouch and Wray's

Founded 1720, rebuilt 1823, funded by Zouch and Wray.
Residents: 4 F (sharing in pairs) Pension.
Refs: CC, v, pp. 459, 465–6.

86. SEDBERGH •

The Widows' Hospital

On Palmer Hill, off the main street, grid ref. SD 655 922.
Founded 1848 by Thomas Palmer.
Low stone row, courses alternately light and dark, overhanging roof of graduated stone slates.
Unadorned. Garden; wash house now demolished.
Residents: 6 F, C of E, of legitimate birth.
Refs: CC, ii, pp. 679, 700; CA. WDEC 18/2, 3; Cann, 2003, pp. 33–41; Cann, 2004, pp. 46–54.

87. SELBY •

Audus and Feoffee Square Almshouses

On Gowthorpe, A63, within the town and houses of the same period, grid ref. SE 610 324.
Founded as two separate charities, Feoffees 1822 and Audus 1833, administered jointly by the feoffees.
Two adjacent courtyards, both open-ended, one paved, one garden, facing the street. Brick, two storey, unadorned, almost identical save for stone door and window heads in Audus and a modest Gothic gateway over the through passage to shared yard.
Plaques: 'These houses built by the Feoffees of Selby 1822' and 'These houses erected at the sole expense of James Audus esq, were presented to the feoffees and their successors at Selby in trust for Poor Uses that the said houses be occupied from time to time by aged and infirm people, without families, belonging to the parish of Selby, rent-free.

Natalis loci amoris monumentum. 1833'.
Residents: 10F + 10(usually)F, local.
Refs: CC, iv, pp. 730, 737; Morrell, 1867.

88. SELBY

Chamberlaine's Hospital

Founded 1716 by Leonard Chamberlain of Hull, rebuilt 1889, linked to school.
Residents: 5 (6) F (M/F), usually nonconformist. Pension, fuel.
Refs: CC, iv, pp. 745, 749–50; Morrell, 1867.

Fig. 79 Audus and Feoffee Square Almshouses at Selby: a) the Audus courtyard with its crenellated tower above the passageway; b) rear view from the drying green of the backs of the two adjacent foundations. *Photos: author.*

Fig. 80 Freeman's Hospital, Sheffield, where the reading room contributes an idiosyncratic central feature to the low stone row. *Photo: author.*

89. SHEFFIELD
Firth's Almshouses
On Nethergreen Road at Ranmoor.
Founded 1869 by Mark Firth, steel manufacturer and cutler, and rebuilt about a century later.
Original building included a chapel, with chaplain, preferably Methodist New Connection, to look after the residents, act as clerk to the trustees and 'do nothing else without their consent'.
Dedicatory stained glass window and plaques from former chapel preserved in modern communal building.
Residents: 36 M/F, Sheffield.
Refs: CC, i, pp. 695–700; The Builder, 1867, p. 396; Kelly, vol. iii, 1904, p. 32.

90. SHEFFIELD •
Freeman's Hospital
On Burncross Road at Chapeltown (formerly Ecclesfield), grid ref. SK 354 964.
Founded 1836 by Lydia Mackereth Freeman.
Single storey stone row with slate roof, symmetrical with unifying string course. Remarkable castellated central unit formed the reading room.
Lozenge-shaped plaque 'Dum spiro spero 1837'; below inscribed 'Reading Room'. Car park may have been garden.
Residents: 6 F, C of E, preferably from the northern end of Ecclesfield. Pension. Non-resident reader.
Rules include repairs.
Now solicitors' offices.
Refs: CC, i, pp. 181–4.

91. SHEFFIELD
Hollis's Hospital
Founded 1703 by Thomas Hollis during his lifetime; trust set up by his son in 1726 and rebuilt 1776.
Original building called the 'great hall', purpose-built replacement a two storey Georgian building with one central door, pediment and plaque.
Rebuilt 1903 by the corporation on Hollis land at Whirlow Bridge in 'a reposeful setting'; three ranges about a courtyard.
Residents: 16 M/F with 1 M 'to read scriptures, pray with the family and visit the sick', later designated the orator; nonconformist. Pension, coal, gowns. Later, cutlers or their widows first choice.
Refs: CC, i, pp. 433–6, 596–606; Baines, 1822, p. 290; Hunter, 1819, pp. 318–19; Kelly, vol. iii, 1904, p. 32; Sheffield Daily Telegraph, 1931; Sheffield Weekly News, 1904.

92. SHEFFIELD •
Sheffield and Rotherham Licensed Victuallers Association Asylum
Woodland View on Abbeydale Road South, Abbeydale, grid ref. SK 323 814.
Founded 1853 at Grimesthorpe, moved to present site 1879.
Single storey stone row enhanced by projecting two storey gabled wings; slate roof. Central chapel with spire. Hood moulds, mullions, traceried windows and dormers in wings. Raised above road with lawn and drive.
Obelisk on lawn inscribed to: 'Alderman Thomas Wiley by the voluntary subscriptions

Fig. 81 The Licensed Victuallers' Asylum, Sheffield, where the central chapel is capped with a spire. *Photo: author.*

of the members and friends of the Sheffield and Rotherham Licensed Victuallers Association to record their respect and esteem for his munificent donation to their asylum he being the first donor to this institution and by his spirited example causing a number of liberal and benevolent gentlemen to subscribe sufficient funds to erect the adjoining buildings. AD 1853. This monument was removed from the old institution at Grimesthorpe to its present site on the completion of these buildings 1879.'

Residents: 8 M/F/C, local, former publicans. Pension.

Refs: Pawson and Brailsford, 1864, 1879; Sheffield History Reporter, 1996.

93. SHEFFIELD •
Earl of Shrewsbury's Hospital

On Norfolk Road, high ground but still central, grid ref. SK 369 875.

Founded 1625 by Gilbert, Earl of Shrewsbury, and built in 1673 by his grandson. Rebuilt after the flood in 1768, in which 4 almspeople drowned. Rebuilt 1823 on present site, opposite typhoid monument. Later nineteenth-century additions and modern almshouses alongside in 6 acre estate.

Complex three-sided courtyard, single storey but incorporating two storey chaplain's house and porter's lodge as well as two storey almshouses in rear wings accessed from Talbot Place. Stone, graduated slate roof, paired porches and chimneys, gently Gothic. Chapel central, relatively plain. Gardens with trees, stone wall with railings and wrought iron gates with device of crossed arrows.

Residents: 20, increased to 36 M/F, Sheffield, any denomination. Pension, fuel, uniform (blue for everyday, purple for best, with a silver badge, later buttons). Governor/chaplain, porter.

Refs: CC, i, pp. 432, 460–73, 565–96; SA. ACM/S 533/7–9; TC 142–4; Hunter, 1819, pp. 314–18; Pevsner, 1967, p. 467; Roach, 2003; White, 1837, p. 89.

Fig. 82 Earl of Shrewsbury's Hospital, Sheffield. a) The wrought iron gates at the entrance. b) Four of the earliest units on this site, from 1823. c) The 1930s interpretation of the row with each porch graced by an individual shield. d) The extensive site accommodated further building in 1964 with clusters of square buildings providing additional units and communal facilities. *Photos: author.*

Fig. 83 George Woofindin Almshouses, Sheffield. These are amongst the largest and latest in foundation. The substantial two storey buildings are surmounted by clusters of tall chimneys; the central range (on the right) houses the communal area. The lawn leads to a shrubbery and flowing stream, beyond which lies the city centre. *Photo: author.*

94. SHEFFIELD •
George Woofindin Almshouses, now Houses
Founded 1895, built 1899 on Eccleshall Road at Hunters Bar, grid ref. SK 332 857.
Three ranges of 6 plus a pair forming a crescent. Brick with darker diaper pattern, two storey with gablets and three-light windows. Central range larger with pediment and communal space. Set in gardens with a stream and shrubbery.
Residents: 18 M/F. Reading room.
Refs: CC, i, pp. 700–2; Kelly, 1904, vol. iii, p. 34.

95. SNAITH
Lord Downe's Almshouses
On Beast Fair, grid ref. SE 644 222.
Founded or rebuilt 1802, demolished 1962.
Single storey row of 6 units, each one room and lean-to.
Residents: 6 F. Pension.
Refs: CC, v, p. 504; ER. NCH/164/1; Noble, 1988, p. 96; Snaith and District Heritage Society, 1990.

96. SNAITH
Snaith Hospital, formerly the Bedehouse
On Cross Hill, the oldest part of the village, grid ref. SE 640 221.
Founded 1624 by Nicholas Waller, built by executor Edmund Yarburgh. Rebuilt 1770, extended 1860s with addition of first floor.
Residents: 3, later, 6 M. Pension.
Refs: CC, v, pp. 486, 502–6; ER. NCH/38/1; Jordan, 1961, p. 271; Noble, 1988, pp. 95–6; Snaith and District Heritage Society, 1990.

97. SOWERBY, near Halifax
Elkana Horton's Almshouses
In the village centre, replaced by a 1960s shopping parade, grid ref. SE 042 233.
Founded 1728 and rebuilt 1861 by Colonel Rawson who bought the estate.
Residents: 3 M + 3 F, Sowerby. Pension. Originally almsmen read prayers in the attached oratory.
Refs: CC, iii, pp. 241, 505–7.

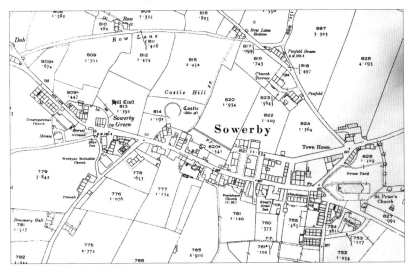

Fig. 84 Elkana Horton's Almshouses stood at the centre of Sowerby, next to the King's Head Inn. *Ordnance Survey, Sheet 55, 1919.*

Fig. 85 Joseph Smith's Almshouses, Thornton-in-Craven: the plaque recording Joseph and Rachel Smith's foundation for five poor women. *Photo: author.*

98. SWILLINGTON, east of Leeds
Swillington Almshouses
Founded 1728 by Lother family. Church and empty school all that remain of old village.
Residents: 4 F. Pension
Refs: CC, v, 542–4.

99 TADCASTER
The Hospital, sometimes called Christ's Hospital
Founded 1559 by Owen Oglethorpe jointly with a school.
Intended as a foundation for 12 almsmen, with dining hall and kitchen, grey uniform, pension and use of the master's orchard, but the school got the larger share.
Residents: 4 M/F. Pension. Resident schoolmaster.
Refs: CC, iv, pp. 789–93, 799; Speight, no date.

100. THORNTON-IN-CRAVEN •
Joseph Smith's Almshouses
On Church Road among fields at the edge of the village, grid ref. SD 905 485.
Founded 1815 by Rachel and Joseph Smith.
Single storey stone row with stone slates, symmetrical and unadorned except for the central Classical pediment. Two room units. Small gardens.
Plaque records 'Joseph Smith, Banker, late of the City of London and native of this parish, and residuary estate of Rachel Smith, his widow'.
Residents: 5 F, local. Pension, fuel, clothing and use of communal kitchen.
Refs: CC, ii, pp. 798, 804; Pevsner, 1967, p. 512.

101. THURNSCOE
The Almshouses
Founded 1710 by the rector.
The cottages faced south, gardens sloping to the brook with fruit trees, vegetables and flowers.
Residents: 3 F/C. Pension.
Refs: CC, I, pp. 844–46.

102. TICKHILL
Maison Dieu and Scarborough Almshouses
In the church precinct, secluded, grid ref. SK 591 931.
Foundation dates uncertain, replaced 1980s. Two separate charities in adjacent buildings, possibly incorporating St. Leonard's Hospital.
Residents: 8 + 5 M/F. Pension, fuel.
Refs: CC, i, pp. 847–8, 851–4; Pevsner, 1967, p.521; VCH, 1913, pp. 332–3; White, 1837, p. 300.

103. WADDINGTON, near Clitheroe •
Waddington Hospital
In the village, beside the river, grid ref. SD 729 441.
Founded 1701 by Robert Parker of Browsholme Hall, rebuilt 1893.
Three-sided courtyard of single storey stone houses with steeply pitched slate roof, moderate chimneys and half-timbered porches. Chapel centrally placed opposite entrance, adjacent row stopped by nurse's home on one side and library and dispensary on the other. Mainly unadorned. Large formal garden with water pump and segments of inscription. Previous building a long row, close behind the pump, in two parts with chapel. Laundry and wash house.
Residents: 20 F, increased to 30 (originally 10), local parishes. Pension, medical care, birthday sermon and dinner on founder's day. Resident nurse, part-time reader in house across the road.
Refs; CC, ii, pp. 565, 577–81; TC/CL; Anon. 1815; Bridge, 1994, pp. 142–155; Pevsner, 1967, p. 525.

Fig. 86 Waddington Hospital. a) The earliest view of the previous building is this 1815 engraving of a unified row, albeit with four units on one side of the recessed chapel and ten on the other. b) This undated photograph differs from the engraving in giving the chapel a round rather than ogee-headed door, while the row to the left has hood moulds over doors and windows although the string course persists to the right. Several building and reconstruction phases may be implied, as may a degree of artistic licence in the engraving. c) A postcard view, photographed by E. Buck of Clitheroe, shortly before the rebuild. d) The central range of the 1893 building housed the nurse and the dispensary in the two storey unit. e) One of the long side ranges seen across the garden with a more recent extension to the left. *Clitheroe Library, Anon., 1815, History of Browsholme (a); Clitheroe Library/Trustee Collection (b and c); photos: author (d and e).*

Fig. 87 Hannah Rawson's Almshouses, Wadsley. Detail of the central feature in which the stepped gable forms a pattern with the hood mould above the passage. The plaque contains a Biblical quotation rather than the founder's name. *Photo: author.*

104. WADSLEY •
Hannah Rawson's Almshouses

Off Worrall Road, at right angles; originally part of Ecclesfield, grid ref. SK 320 906.
Founded 1840

Single storey stone row, symmetrical with projecting bays, passageway through central gabled unit; end units projecting with enclosed porches built into the return. Stepped gables, arched hood moulds and drip moulds give a more Elizabethan than truly Gothic feel. Each unit two rooms, side by side except at ends where one room behind the other. Gardens.

Plaque over central arch 'thus said the Lord "and even to your old age I am He" Isa xl vi 4'.

Residents: 6 F, local, C of E. Pension, fuel.

Refs: CC, i, pp. 201–4; TC.

105. WAKEFIELD •
Major Barker's Homes

On Holmefield Avenue, Thornes, originally the edge of Barker's estate, now part of town, grid ref. SE 325 194.
Founded 1887.

Single storey stone row, projecting central bay with

Fig. 88 Major Barker's Homes, Wakefield: a) the stone row featuring a large window of diverse and eclectic style for each unit, with a neat porch at each end; b) no longer on the perimeter of the founder's estate, the Dutch gable appears behind 1970s garages, whilst the gardenless façade fronts onto an unmade residential street. *Photos: author.*

pediment covered with fluted pilasters, flowers in urns and blank tablets. Ends have inset porches; Dutch gables in between with stone coping. Eclectic style similar to [68] and [110].
Residents: 4 F, local, C of E preferred. Pension.
Refs: CC, v, pp. 700 -1; Taylor, 1976, p. 45.

106. WAKEFIELD

Corporation Almshouses, Thornes
Founded 1853, opposite [105], next to school.
Residents: 4 F.
Refs: CC, v, p. 700.

107. WAKEFIELD •

Cotton Horne's Almshouses
On Horne Street, off A636, part of residential terraced housing of same period, grid ref. SE 319 202.
Founded 1646 and 1669 as separate male and female charities, then amalgamated. Rebuilt 1793, extended 1829 and rebuilt on present site 1901.
Two storey Accrington brick, slate roof, railed gallery for first floor access. Central tower with stairs and passageway. Windows with stone facings, but overall plain and institutional in character, despite trustees' visit to Aberford and Selby before building.
Plaque (from previous building) 'Mr. Cotton Horne erected almshouses for 10 poor men and 10 poor women and gave them for their maintenance £54 7s. 0d. p. a. It is now £200 p. a. Rebuilt in 1793'.
Foundation stone: 'This stone was laid on 15 May 1901 by Alfred William Stanfield esq, spokesman of the governors of the Wakefield charities'.
Residents: 10 M + 10 F, local. Resident nurse (formerly 1 M + 1 F). Pension, clothing, food.
Refs: CC, v, pp. 579–81, 637–40; Banks, 1871, pp. 98–100; Taylor, 1976, pp. 44–5; White, 1837, p. 335.

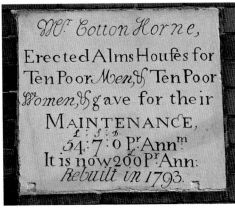

Fig. 89 Cotton Horne's Almshouses, Wakefield. The plaque retained from the previous building proudly states the value of the endowment available for maintenance, including the almspeople's pensions, from foundation until 1793. *Photo: author.*

108. WAKEFIELD •

Caleb Crowther's Almshouses
On George Street, city centre, near former Cotton Horne site, grid ref. SE 330 205.
Founded 1838 by Dr. Crowther, general practitioner and consultant to the pauper lunatic asylum.
Symmetrical stone row, single storey but two in the centre; high pitched slate roof. Gothic doors and windows under drip moulds, quatrefoil motif and curly bargeboards. End of row turns corner to Thornhill Street and the back yard where Dr. Crowther is buried.
Residents: 12 (in 6 units), nonconformist. Pension.
Refs: CC, v, pp. 659–663; JG. Crowther letter, 1839; Banks, 1871; Taylor, 1976, pp. 42–3; Whiteley, 1888.

Fig. 90 Caleb Crowther's Almshouses, Wakefield. Despite his knowledge of human nature, the founder intended two almsmen to share each of these units. *Photo: author.*

NAME OF CHARITY.	**NAMES OF REPRESENTATIVES.**	**PARTICULARS OF CHARITIES.**	Parishes to which Charity applies.	Persons in receipt of Out-Relief and Charity Allowance.	AMOUNT OF OUT-RELIEF.	AMOUNT OF CHARITY.
					WEEKLY.	
1. { DR. CROWTHER'S ALMSHOUSE CHARITY. / G. E. SMITH'S CHARITY.	Mr. F. Firth, 177, Kirkgate. / Mr. J. H. Cameron, New Scarboro'. (Secretary : Mr. Alfred Pickard).	14 Almshouses, 8 in George Street (Dr. Crowther's). 6 in Westfield Road (G. E. Smith's). 2 occupied by married couples; allowance, 9/- each couple ; coal, gas and water free. 12 occupied by single persons; allowance 6/- each, coal, gas, and water free. No regulation as to recipients of Poor Law Relief.	Wakefield.	—	—	
2. THOMAS CLAYTON'S TRUST.	Mr. R. Wallis, Cross Square. Mr. B. S. Briggs, King Street. (Secretary : Mr. Alfred Pickard).	Annual Income £569 9s. 6d. £280 paid out in sums of £5 to each Annuitant half-yearly (£10 yearly). Persons to be 60 years of age or over. Not available to persons in receipt of Poor Law Relief.	Wakefield.	1 Female.	4/6.	£5 half-yearly.
3. JOSEPH MARSLAND'S ALMS-HOUSES.	Mr. R. Wallis, Cross Square. Mr. Geo. Micklethwaite, Legh Street. (Secretary : Mr. Alfred Pickard).	9 Almshouses. Each occupied by one woman who receives £6 yearly by quarterly instalments. Coal, gas, and water free. Persons to be 60 years of age or over. No regulation as to recipients of Poor Law Relief.	Wakefield.	4 Females.	2/6 each.	£6 per annum and Alms-house.
4. JOSEPH HARRISON'S CHARITY.	Dr. W. A. Statter. Rev. J. N. Soden. Mr. Chalker. (Clerks : Messrs. Stewart & Chalker).	Pension of £10 per annum to 20 poor men or women. The Trustees treat Alms Persons and Pensioners of other Charities as disqualified, but very deserving cases in receipt of Poor Law Relief are not con-sidered as disqualified.	Wakefield.	1 Female. 1 Female. Man and Wife.	3/6. 7/6. 2/6.	£10 per annum Do. Do.
5. SARAH HARRISON'S CHARITY.	Dr. W. A. Statter. Rev. J. N. Soden. Mr. Chalker. (Clerks : Messrs. Stewart & Chalker).	Pension of £10 per annum to 10 poor men or women, payable half-yearly. As to persons in receipt of Poor Law Relief, same as Joseph Harrison's Charity.	Wakefield.	—	—	—
6. LADY HUTCHINSON'S CHARITY.	Mr. C. B. L. Fernandes, Secretary.	Pension of about £10 per annum to 6 poor Cloth Workers. No regulation as to recipients of Poor Law Relief.	Wakefield.	—	—	—
7. WAKEFIELD CORPORATION.	(Clerk : Mr. W. W. Greenhalgh).	6 Almshouses at Thornes.	Wakefield.	1 Female.	3/-.	10/- per month from Brother-ton's Charity Trust and resides in Corporation Almshouse.
8. MAJOR BARKER'S HOMES.	(Secretary : Mr. F. J. Munby, Blake Street, York).	4 Almshouses for poor women, who also receive a pension of 5/- per week.	Wakefield.	—	—	—
9. BROTHERTON CHARITY TRUST.	Mr. John Lumpy	10	Wakefield.			

Fig. 91 Data gathered by the Wakefield Union: Outdoor Relief and Charitable Funds in 1908. Shortly before the introduction of the state old age pension, eligibility for poor law relief by the beneficiaries of almshouse and other charities remained a vexed issue. (Marsland's residents are here noted in a receipt of a pension). *WYAS, W, C547/1/1/5, no. 36.*

109. WAKEFIELD
Marsland's Almshouses
Between John Street and Berners Street, grid ref. SE 335 214.
Founded 1886. Architect F. Simpson, see [68].
Demolished 1983.
The row included a mission house and a house for its caretaker.
Residents: 9 M/F, local, nonconformist. Pension, furniture.
Refs: CC, v, pp. 678–80; Wakefield Express, 1982.

110. WAKEFIELD •
Smith's Almshouses
On Westfield Road, jutting into the school playing fields, grid ref. SE 330 215.
Founded 1887 and built for £1,480.
Red brick with grey slate roof, protruding bays, Dutch gables, pilasters similar to [105]. Small garden.
Plaque on gable end, facing street, 'Homes for the Poor erected and endowed by G E Smith AD 1887. Arnold Nicholson, MSA, Architect'.
Residents: 6 M/F. Pension, furniture.
Refs: CC, v, p. 665.

Fig. 92 Smith's Almshouses, Wakefield. This brick row has three-light windows and decorative gables reminiscent of those at Major Barker's. The building is set end-on to the road, giving the residents an open view across the small garden and school playing fields beyond. *Photo: author.*

Fig. 93 Wentworth Hospital: the founder's coat of arms set into the recently repointed brickwork. *Photo: author.*

111. WENTWORTH •
The Almshouses
Outside the village at Barrow, grid ref. SK 380 985. Founded 1697 by one of the Fitzwilliam family. Courtyard, two storey front range, the other three single storey. Old red brick with three string courses, although the village is mainly stone. Entrance to courtyard through central arch below pediment and small wooden clocktower (restored).
Residents: 12 M/F, 'the eldest and poorest', Wentworth and estate. Pension, clothing, food.
Refs: CC, i, pp. 878–9, 922; Pevsner, p. 545.

112. WHITLEY UPPER, near Lepton
Bedford's Gift
Founded 1767 with money left to the parish poor and demolished late 1890s.
Residents: 4 F.
Refs: CC, iii, pp. 836–7.

113. WHIXLEY
Tancred's Hospital
In its grounds on the old road at the edge of the village, grid ref. SE 456 580.
Founded 1781.
The manor house was adapted after the founder's death to accommodate almsmen, dining room, chapel, supporting staff and Tancred's coffin, which was lead and remained above ground. Later problems may have led to an outpensions charity; the present building is a nursing home.
Residents: 12 M, British, ex-professional or services. Resident caterer and 3 maids. Pension, meals.
Refs: WYAS,Y. DD160.

114. WILSHAW, near Holmfirth •
Eleanor Hirst's Almshouses
On The Avenue, woods behind and fields in front in the dispersed village, grid ref. SE 116 096.
Founded 1871.
Modest semi-detached small stone villas, in a row; two storey with Welsh slate roof and dormers. Paired stone porches, window hood moulds with leaf terminals. Rustic and slightly Italianate. Gardens and drying ground.
Plaque 'These almshouses were erected by Eleanor the beloved wife of Joseph Hirst of this place in loving remembrance of Mary their deeply lamented and only child whose love and sympathy for the poor when living makes these houses intended for the aged and destitute a fitting memorial to an affectionate daughter who was always ready to add comfort to those in want and declining years. AD 1871'.
Residents: 6 M/F, local, former employees first choice. Pension, fuel, furniture.
Refs: CC, iii, pp. 56, 59–61.

115. WOMBWELL •
Victoria Almshouses, formerly Hunshelf's, now Wombwell Townland Charity
On Summer Lane, on the hillside overlooking the cemetery, grid ref. SE 395 031.
Founded 1615, rebuilt and renamed 1888.
Two storey stone row, slate roof, symmetrical with gablets and open porches, plain and local.
Small garden behind stone wall and gate.
Residents; 12 M/F, local, minimum income, miners first choice.
Refs: CC, v, pp. 96–7.

Fig. 94 Victoria Almshouses. The gate to what was once Hunshelf's, then Victoria Almshouses, and is now Wombwell Townland Charity. *Photo: author.*

Addenda

A DONCASTER
Hunt Committee's Almshouses
Founded after 1891.

B KNARESBOROUGH
Hospital
Survey of 1611 records building on Kirkgate as 'hospital for six poor folk'.
Also demolished almshouses near High Bridge, Waterside.

C LEEDS
St. Saviour's Almshouses
On Richmond Hill. Founded 1862, demolished 1942.

D LINDLEY, near Huddersfield
Almshouse Arch
On East Street. Stone doorway inserted into modern porch.

Bibliography

General and other regional works

Books

Almshouse Association. 2003. *Annual Report*, Wokingham: Almshouse Association

Bailey, B. 1988. *Almshouses*, London: Hale

Brunskill, E. 1960. *Some Yorkshire Almshouses*, York: York Georgian Society

Burnett, J. 1986. *A Social History of Housing, 1815–1985*, London: Methuen

Checkland, O. 1980. *Philanthropy in Victorian Scotland : social welfare and the voluntary principle*, Edinburgh: Donald

Clay, R.M. 1909. *The Medieval Hospitals of England*, London: Cass

Cockburn, E. 1970. *The Almshouses of Dorset*, Dorchester: Friary Press

Crust, L. 2002. *Lincolnshire Almshouses: nine centuries of charitable housing*, Sleaford: Heritage of Lincolnshire

Cullum, P. H. 1991. *Cremetts and Corodies: care of the poor and sick at St. Leonard's Hospital in the Middle Ages*, Borthwick Papers 79, York: University of York

Cunningham, H. and Innes, J. 1998. *Charity, Philanthropy and Reform from the 1690s to 1850*, Basingstoke: Macmillan

Darley, G. 1975. *Villages of Vision*, London: Architectural Press

Fraser, D. 2003. *The Evolution of the British Welfare State*, Basingstoke: Macmillan

Girouard, M. 1990. *The English Town*, Yale University Press

Godfrey, W. 1955. *The English Almshouse with some account of its predecessor the Medieval Hospital*, London: Faber

Granshaw, L. and Porter, R. eds. 1990. *The Hospital in History*, London: Routledge

Gray, K. B. 1905. *A History of English Philanthropy*, London: King

Hallett, A. 2004. *Almshouses*, Princes Risborough: Shire

Heath, S. 1910. *Old English Houses of Alms: a pictorial record with architectural and historical notes*, London: Griffiths

Hey, D. 1981. *Buildings of Britain, 1550–1750: Yorkshire*, Ashbourne: Morland

Hobson, J. 1926. *Some early and later Houses of Pity*, London: Routledge

Howson, B. 1993. *Houses of Noble Poverty: a history of the English Almshouse*, Sunbury: Bellevue

Jordan, W. K. 1959. *Philanthropy in England 1480–1660*, London: Allen and Unwin

Jordan, W. K. 1961. *The Charities of Rural England, 1480–1660*, London: Allen and Unwin

Judges, A. V. 1936. *The Elizabethan Underworld*, London

London Housing Centre. 1945. *The London Almshouse: six centuries of housing for the aged*, London: London Housing Centre

McConaghy, M. et al. 2000. *Housing in England 1998–99*, London: Stationery Office

Morris, E. 1996. *Victorian and Edwardian Paintings in the Walker Art Gallery and at Sudley House*, Liverpool: Walker Art Gallery

Morrison, K. 1999. *The Workhouse: a study of Poor Law buildings in England*, London: English Heritage

Orme, N. and Webster, M. 1995. *The English Hospital, 1070–1570*, Yale University Press

Owen, D. 1964. *English Philanthropy 1660–1960*, Harvard and Oxford University Press

Page, R. and Silburn, R. eds. 1998. *British Social Welfare in the twentieth century*, Basingstoke, Macmillan

Pannell, J. and Thomas, C. 1999. *Almshouses into the next millennium: paternalism, partnership, progress?*, Bristol: Policy Press

Pevsner, N. 1967. *Buildings of England: Yorkshire, West Riding*, Harmondsworth: Penguin

Prescott, E. C. 1992. *The English Medieval Hospital 1050–1640*, Seaby

Slack, P. 1990. *The English Poor Law 1531–1782*, Cambridge University Press

Slack, P. 1999. *From Reformation to Improvement:*

public welfare in Early Modern England, Oxford: Clarendon Press

Stearns, P. ed. 1982. *Old Age in Pre-Industrial Society*, New York: Holmes and Meier

Summerson, J. 1970. *Architecture in Britain, 1530–1830*, Harmondsworth: Penguin

Tate Gallery. 2002. *Tate Collections: general collection*, London: Tate Gallery

Thane, P. 2000. *Old Age in English History*, Oxford University Press

Thomson, D. 1991. 'The Welfare of the Elderly in the past', in Pelling, M. and Smith, R. eds. *Life, Death and the Elderly: Historical Perspectives*, London: Routledge

Thompson, F. 1939. *Lark Rise to Candleford*. repr. 1973, Harmondsworth: Penguin

Tompson, R. 1979. *The Charity Commission and the Age of Reform*, London: Routledge

Wilkins, I. 1989. *The Alms Trade: charity past, present and future*, University of London

Articles

Bryson, J., McGuiness, M. and Ford, R. 1999. 'A Thirdway or an Old Way? Almshouse charities and the rise of the post-Welfare State', *Services, Space and Society*, vii, University of Birmingham

Citizens Advice Bureau, 2001. 'A Farewell to Alms', *Housing Matters*, April 2001

Theses

Hunnyball, P. 1994. 'Status, Display and Dissemination: social expression and stylistic change in the architecture of seventeenth-century Hertfordshire', unpublished D. Phil. thesis, University of Oxford

Lambert, S. 1997. 'Seventeenth-century Berkshire Almshouses', unpublished M. Phil. thesis, University of Reading

Prescott, E. C. 1988. 'Medieval Hospitals and Almshouses: the changing scene, c. 1200–1640', unpublished M. Phil. thesis, University of Southampton

Local histories, etcetera

Books and pamphlets

Anon. 2000. *The Time of our Lives in Heath*, published privately

Bell, M. 1987. *Cawood, the History of a Yorkshire Village*, published privately

Bretton, W. no date. *History of Gawber*, Gawber

Bridge, M. 1994. *Waddington Village Life in the Nineteenth Century*, Settle: Hudson

Bulley, J. 1959. *Hemsworth in History*, Hemsworth

Dodd, E. 1958. *Bingley*, Leeds: Rigg

Douglas, J and Powell, K. 1993. *St. John's Church, Leeds*, London: Redundant Churches Fund

Everett, B. no date. *A History of Kirkthorpe*, Publisher unknown

Hargreaves, J. 1999. *Halifax in Old Picture Postcards*, Halifax

Minett, N. no date. 'Methley's Heritage' in Groundwork Leeds, *Settlement Walks of the Lower Aire Valley*, Leeds

Naylor, R. 1992. *Carleton with an 'E'*, Settle: Lambert

Noble, M. ed. 1988. *Life in the Past around Snaith*, Snaith Historical Society

Pacey, A., Bayer, P. et al.. 2001. *Pioneering Science in the Pennines*, W.E.A. Conference Papers, Leeds: W.E.A.

Pearson, E. 1972. 'The Ancient Hospitals' in Ripon Civic Society, *Ripon, some Aspects of its History*, Clapham: Dalesman

Percy, C. 1990. *Beamsley Hospital, notes produced for the Landmark Trust*, Maidenhead: Landmark

Reynolds, J. 1983. *The Great Paternalist*, London: Temple Smith

Roach, J. 2003. *The Shrewsbury Hospital, Sheffield, 1616–1975*, Borthwick Papers 104, York: University of York

Snaith and District Heritage Society. 1990. *Town Trail*, Snaith

Speight, W. no date. *Two Thousand Years of Tadcaster History*, Tadcaster

Spence, R. T. 1997. *Lady Anne Clifford*, Stroud: Sutton

Taylor, K. 1976. *Wakefield District Heritage*, Wakefield Heritage Committee

Victoria County History. 1913. *A History of the County of York*, vol. iii, London: Constable

West Yorkshire Archaeology Service. no date. *Historic Pontefract: information sheet*, Wakefield

White, A. 2004. *Maids and Mistresses*, Leeds City Council

Articles

Bretton, R. 1950–54. 'Crossleys of Dean Clough', *Halifax Antiquarian Society Transactions*, i–iv

Caffrey, H. 2004. 'The Almshouse Experience in the Nineteenth-century West Riding', *Yorkshire Archaeological Society*, 76

Cann, R. 2003–04. 'Sedbergh United Charities and Widows Hospital', *The Sedbergh Historian*, iv, 6, and v,1

Girouard, M. 1970. 'Visions of Halifax', *CountryLife*, September 1970

Halifax Courier. 1965. 'Helping hand', *Halifax Courier*, occasional series

Hustwick, W. 1957–62. 'Odd Corners of Bradford', *Bradford Telegraph and Argus*

Sheffield Library. 1996. 'Lost Buildings of Sheffield', *Sheffield History Reporter*

Newspapers

Guardian, 2001, 14 March
Halifax Daily Courier, 1967, 3 January
Pontefract and Castleford Express, 1982, 29 March
Sheffield Daily Telegraph, 1931, picture series
Sheffield Weekly News, 1904, 14 May
Wakefield Express, 1982, 15 January
Wakefield Express, 2001, 22 June
Yorkshire Post, 1968, 15 February

Theses

Caffrey, H. 2002. 'Almshouses: an enduring Concept of Care', unpublished M.A. dissertation, University of Lancaster
Clayton, J. 1940. 'Waterhouse Charities', unpublished M. A. dissertation, University of Leeds
Cullum, P. 1989. 'Hospitals and Charitable Provision in Medieval Yorkshire 936–1547', unpublished D. Phil. thesis, University of York

Primary sources

Printed works

Anon. 1815. *History of Browsholme*, published privately
Baines, E. 1822. *History of Yorkshire with a Directory of its Inhabitants and a Gazetteer*, Leeds
Banks, W. S. 1862. *Walks in Yorkshire*, Wakefield: Hall
Banks, W.S. 1871. *Walks about Wakefield*, Wakefield
Bibby, J. 1910. *A History of Bentham*, publisher unknown
Booth, C. 1894. *The Aged Poor in England and Wales*, London: Macmillan
Boothroyd, B. 1807. *The History of Pontefract*, Pontefract
Bradford Flower Fund, 1960. *Bradford Flower Fund Homes*, Bradford
Bradford Tradesmen's Benevolent Association. 1915–99. *Annual Reports*, Bradford
Charity Commissioners. 1837. *Reports of the Commissioners in pursuance of Acts of Parliament; 58 Geo iii c 91, 59 Geo iii c 81and 5 Geo iv c 58 to enquire concerning Charities and Education of the Poor in England and Wales*, vol. xl, London
Charity Commissioners. 1897–99. *Endowed Charities: comprising the reports made to the Charity Commissioners subject to the provision of the Charitable Trusts Act 1853–91 together with the reports on those endowments of the charities from enquiries concerning charities 1818–37*, West Riding vols. i–v, London
Cudworth, C. 1891. *History of Bolton and Bowling*, Bradford: Brear
Dawson, H. W. 1882. *History of Skipton*, London: Simpkin, Marshall and Co.
Dickens, C. 1850–59. *Household Words*, repr. 1964, Oxford

Dickens, C. 1860–69. *The Uncommercial Traveller*, 29, repr. 1964, Oxford
Doncaster Gazette. 1900–10. *Doncaster Gazette Directories*, Doncaster
Fletcher, J. 1900. *A Picturesque History of Yorkshire*, London: Dent
Fox, G. 1827. *The History of Pontefract*, Pontefract: Fox
Gilbert Committee. 1816 edn. *Charitable Returns for the Benefit of Poor Persons, 26 Geo iii*, London
Hanson, T. 1920, *The Story of Old Halifax*, repr. 1985, Otley: Smith Settle
Hewitt, J. 1862. *History and Topography of the parish of Wakefield and its Environs*, Wakefield
Hole, J. 1866. *The Homes of the Working Classes*, London
Hunter, J. 1819. *Hallamshire*, London: Virtue
Hunter, J. 1828–31. *South Yorkshire*, repr. 1974, Wakefield: EP
Jackson, C. 1881. *Doncaster Charities Past and Present*, Doncaster
Jefferson, W. et al. 1854. *Report of the Investigation Committee of the Alms-Houses and Miscellaneous charities of the Town of Pontefract*, Pontefract: Fox Copley
Kelly, 1904. *Directory of Leeds and Bradford, vol. ii*, London: Kelly
Kelly, 1904. *Directory of Sheffield and Rotherham, vol. iii*, London: Kelly
Morrell, W. 1867. *History and Antiquities of Selby*, Bellerby
Pawson and Brailsford. 1864, 1879. *Illustrated Guide to Sheffield*, Sheffield
Peacock, T. L. 1831. *Crotchet Castle*, repr. 1986, Harmondsworth: Penguin
Pugin, A. W. N. 1836. *Contrasts*, repr. 1973, Leicester University Press: Victorian Library
Smiles, S. 1877. *Thrift*, London: Murray
Speight, H. 1900. *Upper Wharfedale*, London
Sykes, D. 1910. *The History of Huddersfield*, Huddersfield: Worker Press
Trollope, A. 1855. *The Warden*, repr. 1991, London: Everyman
Watson, J. 1775. *The History and Antiquities of the Parish of Halifax*, Halifax
Whitaker, T. D. 1805. *History and Antiquities of the Deanery of Craven in the County of Yorkshire*, repr. 1973, Skipton
White, W. 1837. *Directory of the West Riding of Yorkshire*, Sheffield: Leader
White, T. 1833. *An Enquiry into the origin and Management of the Hospitals, Almshouses and other Charities of Kingston-upon-Hull*, Hull
Whiteley, R. 1888. *Dr. Crowther's Charities and the Smith Charity, Wakefield*, Wakefield
Wilkinson, J. c. 1869. *Notes and cuttings on Darton and District*, unpublished

Newspapers
Barnsley Civic Review, 1955, 78
Bradford Telegraph and Argus, 1971, 7 April
The Builder, 1847, iv; 1859, xv; 1863, xviv; 1865, xxi; 1867, xxiii

Manuscripts
BA. BB 22/1–8. *Plans, receipts, submissions*
BM 2/1. *Receipts, illustration*
D2. MD 542/1. *Accounts*
BL. B363.5. *Regulations*
CA. WDEC 18/2–3. *Minutes*
DA. DX/War B5. *Minutes*
B12. *Plans*
D2, MD 542/1. *Illustration*
ER. DDCL/560. *New Scheme, outpensions*
NCH/164/1; NCH/38/1. *Accounts*
HU. DDCA (2) 11/13, 14; DDCA 4/ 123, 125. *Deeds, drafts*
JG. Unnumbered. *Minutes, memorabilia, founder's letter*
LL. www.leodis.net. *Photographs*
NY. DC/RIC ix 2/5/9–13; DC/RIC ix 6/1. *Scheme, plans*
PR/BNA 17/4/1–7. *Correspondence, register*
PR/BNL 11/5. *Report*
PR/PRL 17/5, 6. *Accounts, correspondence*
PR/PRL 18/8/17–19, 24. *Minutes, accounts*
PR/PRL 18/9/4–7. *Minutes, correspondence*
RALS. 167/T/1; 167/T2/1. *Constitution, correspondence*
RL. Y/362 900. *Notes, cuttings*
SA. ACM/S 533/7–9; TC 142–4. *Minutes, correspondence, admissions*
TC. Joseph Crossley's Almshouse; Archbishop Holgate's Hospital; Frieston and Sagar's Hospitals; Hannah Rawson's Almshouses; Waddington Hospital. *Minutes, plans, correspondence, illustrations*
WYAS,B. B363. *Regulations*
29D 87/71; 68D 95/1. *Transfer, plans*
62D99/3/5/2. *Plans*
WYAS,C. BIP/HX 298; 666. *Plans*
FW 34/41, 46, 48. *Deed, correspondence*
HAS 672/42–49. *Bonds*
HX T626, 627. *Accounts*
HX 672/42–49. *Bonds*
HX Misc. 96a. *Indenture, decree*
Misc. 129. *Family*
Misc. 137/18–65, 66–91. *Negotiations, plans*
Misc. 703/15. *Drawing*
NOR 19. *Sale*
NOR 20/1, 2. *Objects*
WYAS,K. H Misc. 362. *Outpensions*
KC 627/3/1. *Plan*
KC 643/1/1. *Deed*
KC 643/2/1, 2. *Accounts*
KC 644. *Map, plans*
KC 992/ 1–3. *Minutes*
SC 13/143. *Pensioners*
S/HC Box 115/6/7/11,12. *Deeds, pensions*
WYAS 263/4/1. *Reports, payments*
WYAS 263/5/1. *Trustees*
WYK 1086/1/1–6. *Deed, constitution*
WYAS,L. GA/A9. *Deed*
GA/2/26. *Indenture, history, report*
WYL 1002 acc.2379. *Rules*
Uncatalogued. *Accounts, minutes*
WYAS,W. C 345/1/1–6. *Minutes*
C 345/1/17. *Scheme*
C 345/1/20. *Register*
C 345/1/26. *Chronicle*
C 345/1/43. *Applications*
C 345/3/1. *Interrogations*
C 493/15, 37. *Accounts*
C 493/67–70. *Applications*
C 547/2/5/1. *Survey*
C 547/4/1/1. *Gilbert return*
C 547/4/1/5. *Correspondence*
D 75/91. *Constitution, parish accounts*
WYAS,Y. DD58. *Will*
DD139. *Founder's report*
DD154. *Wills*
DD160/8–10. *Regulations, pensions*

Fig. 95 The gateway from St. Thomas's Hospital, Doncaster, with its lintel inscription, has been preserved and re-erected off Chequer Road after the demolition of the almshouses. *Photo: author.*